Viva Avocado

Celebrating the Perfect Food

Nicholas J. Webb

Published by
Lassen Scientific, Inc.

Viva Tortilla is a Trademark of Lassen Scientific, Inc.

Copyright © 2006 by Nicholas J. Webb

ISBN: 1-59971-638-0

For more information visit

Lassen Scientific, Inc.
www.lassenscientific.com
www.vivatortilla.com

Table of Contents

The Avocado, The Perfect Food

The avocado began its distinguished history sometime between 7,000 B.C. and 5,000 B.C. in south-central Mexico. Archaeologists in Peru have found domesticated avocado seeds buried with Incan mummies dating back to 750 B.C.

Avocados took their name from Spanish conquistadors who adored their taste but could not pronounce the difficult Aztec name, ahuacatl. They changed it to aguacate which eventually evolved into avocado in English. This fruit has been known by many names. In Chile, Peru and Ecuador it is called Palta. In West Africa it is called the custard apple. In Spain it is known as abogado; in France avocat.

The first avocado tree planted in North America was in Florida in 1833 but this increasingly popular fruit would eventually take root in California. The first trees were planted in Santa Barbara, California in 1871 and today 95 percent of the U.S. crop of avocados are grown in California. According to the California Avocado Commission, most California avocados are harvested on 60,000 acres between San Luis Obispo and the Mexican border.

Many believe the avocado to be a vegetable, due to its color and common uses in soups and salads. In reality, it is categorized as a fruit. In botany, a fruit is the ripened ovary, together with the seeds of a flowering plant. When discussing cuisine, fruit foods are usually thought to be just plant fruits that are sweet and fleshy, such as apples, oranges and plums. In reality, many common vegetables, as well as nuts and grains, fall into this category. The avocado is among this group.

The USDA praises the virtues of the avocado. Nutritionally, it leads all other fruits in amounts of beta-carotene and exceeds even the banana in potassium. Most other fruits gain sugar as they ripen; the avocado's sugar content decreases with maturity. At one time the avocado was criticized for its high fat content. Now research has shown that avocados contain "good" unsaturated fats that do not raise blood cholesterol and have been shown to promote higher nutrient absorption when combined with other fruits and vegetables.

New research suggests that avocados may even lower cholesterol levels due to their natural ability to provide beta-sitosterol, a compound that has been widely prescribed as an anti-cholesterol drug that interferes with cholesterol absorption, thus promoting lower cholesterol levels.

It also contains more protein, potassium, magnesium, folic acid, thiamine, riboflavin, niacin, biotin, pantothenic acid, Vitamin E and Vitamin K per ounce than any other fruit.

With its smooth, nutty flavor, the avocado is a virtual powerhouse of health. Most commonly avocados are found in soups, salads and dips. Other cultures have enjoyed many diverse dishes using the avocado; ice creams, sorbets, drinks, breads and pastries to name a few. Viva Avocado has compiled a delectable number of dishes spotlighting this amazing fruit; the avocado, the perfect food.

California Avocado Commission
Tips of Fruit Selection and Handling

Selecting Fresh Fruit

- When selecting an avocado, look for the Fresh California Avocado brand, your assurance that the fruit was grown under optimal conditions.
- The best way to tell if a California avocado is ready for immediate use is to gently squeeze the fruit in the palm of your hand. Ripe, ready-to-eat fruit will be firm yet will yield to gentle pressure.
- Color alone may not tell the whole story. The Hass avocado will turn dark green or black as it ripens, but other varieties retain their light-green skin even when ripe.
- If you plan to serve the fruit in a few days, stock up on hard, unripened fruit.
- Avoid fruit with dark blemishes on the skin.

Ripening a California Avocado

- To ripen a California avocado, place the fruit in a plain brown paper bag and store at room temperature until ready to eat (usually two to five days).
- Including an apple or banana in the bag accelerates the process because these fruits give off ethylene gas, a ripening reagent.
- Ripe fruit can be refrigerated until it is eaten, but not for more than two or three days.
- The California Avocado Commission does not recommend using a microwave to accelerate the ripening process.

Handling California Avocados

As with any food preparation, begin by washing your hands in hot, soapy water and dry them with a clean paper towel.

To avoid cross-contamination from raw meat, poultry or eggs, always disinfect your cutting surfaces and utensils.

Thoroughly wash the fruit before you slice it.

Peeling a California Avocado

Use this simple three-step process:

1. Start with a ripe avocado and cut it lengthwise around the seed. Rotate the halves to separate.
2. Remove the seed by sliding the tip of a spoon gently underneath and lifting out. The other common seed-extraction method - striking the seed with a knife - is dangerous and not recommended.
3. Peel the fruit by placing the cut side down and removing the skin with a knife or your fingers, starting at the small end. Or simply scoop out the avocado meat with a spoon. Be sure to sprinkle all cut surfaces with lemon or lime juice or white vinegar to prevent discoloration.

Storing or freezing California Avocados

Ripe fruit can be stored in the refrigerator uncut for two to three days.
To store cut fruit, sprinkle it with lemon or lime juice or white vinegar and place it in an air-tight covered container in your refrigerator. Eat within a day or two.
If refrigerated guacamole turns brown during storage, simply discard the top, browned layer.
When you have an abundance of fresh fruit, consider freezing it. Although avocados are not satisfactorily frozen whole or sliced, pureed avocados freeze very well and can be used in salads, sandwiches and dips.

- Wash, seed and peel the fruit as described above.
- Puree the flesh, adding one tablespoon of lemon juice for each two pureed avocados. Pack the puree into a rigid container, leaving 1 inch of headspace.
- Seal and label the containers.
- Freeze and use within four to five months.

Soups

Avocado Soup

2 ripe avocados, peeled, pitted and sliced
4 c cold chicken broth (can substitute vegetable broth for vegetarian)
2 Tbl fresh lime juice
1/2 tsp cayenne pepper
Salt and freshly ground black pepper to taste

Mash avocados in a food processor until they form a smooth paste. Add the paste to the chicken/vegetable broth, stirring until well mixed. Add remaining ingredients and mix thoroughly. Salt and freshly ground black pepper to taste. Refrigerate for at least 1 hour before serving. Garnish with fresh chives, more diced avocados and serve cold.

Makes 2 servings.

Vegan Avocado Soup

1 small red onion, chopped finely
1 Tbl olive oil
1 ripe avocado, peeled, pitted and sliced
2 tsp soy sauce
2 1/2 c water
Sea salt
Freshly ground black pepper

Sauté onion in olive oil over medium/high heat until it is transparent. Combine onion, avocado, soy sauce and water in food processor. Blend until smooth. Pour mixture into a small saucepan and heat over medium heat until boiling. Reduce heat and simmer for 2 to 3 minutes. Sea salt and freshly ground black pepper to taste. Serve immediately.

Makes 1 serving.

Chilled Chipotle Avocado Soup

4 oz low-fat sour cream
2 ripe avocados, peeled, pitted and sliced
6 3/4 oz green chilies
1/2 Tbl garlic powder
1/2 quart light cream
1 c heavy cream
1/2 c red onion, diced
1 oz Chipotle chili
1 c whole milk
Salt and white pepper to taste

Puree avocados, green chilies, red onion and Chipotle chili in food processor or blender. Combine all ingredients in a mixing bowl and mix well. Salt and white pepper to taste. Refrigerate overnight and serve chilled.

Makes 4 servings.

Avocado and Crab Meat Soup

1 can low-free cream of chicken soup
1 c light cream
1 tsp white onion, minced
1 tsp dried parsley
1/4 tsp salt
Dash of black pepper
1 (7 1/2 oz) can crab meat, drained and washed
2 tsp fresh lemon juice
1 ripe avocado, peeled, pitted and diced

Combine all ingredients except avocado in a medium saucepan and cook over medium/low heat. When soup bubbles around the edges, add avocados and heat thoroughly. Serve immediately.

Makes 4 servings.

Creamy Avocado Soup

2 ripe avocados, peeled, pitted and sliced
1 1/2 c plain soy milk, warmed to room temperature
1 (4oz) can green peppers
1 medium white onion, chopped
1 Tbl fresh cilantro, chopped
Salt and freshly ground black pepper to taste
2 tsp fresh lemon juice
2 tsp dry sherry
Chopped chilies or fresh parsley to garnish

Puree avocados in blender or food processor until smooth. Add soy milk, green peppers, onion and cilantro and puree until creamy. Salt and black pepper to taste, then add lemon juice and sherry. Garnish with chopped chilies or fresh parsley. Serve immediately.

Makes 2 servings.

Chilled Cucumber and Avocado Soup

1 fresh cucumber, peeled seeded and chopped
1 ripe Haas avocado, peeled, pitted and chopped
2 green onions, chopped
2 Tbl fresh lime juice
1 c low-fat sour cream
1 c cold water
Sea salt and freshly ground black pepper
2 Tbl fresh cilantro, chopped

In a blender or food processor, combine cucumber, avocado, green onions, lime juice, sour cream and water. Process until smooth. Season to taste with sea salt and black pepper. Soup can be thinned with water if needed.
Stir in cilantro and serve immediately. Can also serve chilled.

Makes 4 servings.

California Avocado Poblano Soup

2 Tbl tomato, diced finely
2 Tbl green onion, thinly sliced
1/3 Tbl plus 2 tsp fresh lime juice, divided
2 lbs California avocados, peeled and pitted
3 c white onion, chopped
2 1/4 c yellow bell pepper, chopped
3/4 c Poblano chili, chopped
3 Tbl garlic, chopped
2 tsp vegetable oil
1 c dry white wine
2 quarts water or chicken stock
2 tsp ground cumin
12 cilantro sprigs
Queso fresca or feta cheese, crumbled for garnish
Deep fried tortilla strips for garnish

To make garnish, mix tomato, green onion, 2 tsp lime juice, and a large pinch of salt. Reserve.

To make soup, dice avocado. Mix with remaining 1/3 Tbl lime juice; reserve. Sauté onion, peppers and garlic in oil over high heat until lightly browned, about 5 minutes. De glaze pan with wine, reduce by half. Add water or stock, cumin, chili powder, pepper and salt. Simmer, covered, for 1 hour.

Puree mixture with reserved avocado mixture and cilantro sprigs; thin to desired consistency with additional water or stock.

Add additional salt if necessary.

Serve hot soup garnished with 1tsp cheese, 1 tsp reserved tomato mixture and a few broken tortilla chips.

Makes 12 servings.

This recipe is courtesy the California Avocado Commission.

Garlic Avocado Soup

2 ripe avocados, peeled, pitted and cubed
1 clove garlic, crushed
3 c chicken broth (can substitute vegetable broth for vegetarian)
1 Tbl fresh lime juice
1 Tbl low-fat sour cream
Salt and freshly ground black pepper to taste
Hot pepper sauce to taste
Fresh chives, chopped finely for garnish

Combine avocados, garlic 1 1/2 c chicken broth, lime juice and sour cream in blender or food processor. Puree until smooth.
Mix in remaining chicken broth, blending until smooth. Salt, pepper and hot pepper sauce to taste. Chill soup for 1 hour before serving. Garnish with chives.

Makes 4 to 5 servings.

California Avocado Bisque Soup

3 quarts milk
1/3 c fresh tarragon leaves, chopped
1Tbl salt
12 California avocados
1/2 c fresh lemon juice
1/4 tsp cayenne pepper, or to taste
Sour cream, as needed for garnish

Combine milk, tarragon and salt in a large saucepan and bring to a simmer. (Do not boil) Remove from heat and let stand for 1 hour.

Meanwhile puree avocados and lemon juice in a blender until smooth. When milk is ready, whisk in avocado mixture; stir in cayenne. Chill at least 2 hours to marry flavors. To serve chilled, garnish one cup of soup with swirl of sour cream. To serve hot, heat one cup of soup, garnish with a swirl of sour cream. Makes 24 servings.

This recipe is courtesy of the California Avocado Commission.

Chicken and Lime Avocado Soup

4 corn tortillas, julienned
1 1/2 Tbl extra-virgin olive oil
1 white onion, sliced thinly
6 cloves garlic, sliced thinly
4 fresh jalapeños, sliced
8 oz skinless, boneless chicken breast halves, cut into thin strips
1 quart chicken broth
1/4 c fresh lime juice
1 tomato, seeded and diced
Salt and freshly ground black pepper to taste
1 avocado, peeled, pitted and diced
1/4 c fresh cilantro, chopped

Preheat oven to 400 degrees F. Arrange tortilla strips on a baking sheet and bake in preheated oven until lightly browned, about 3 to 5 minutes. In a large saucepan over medium heat, cook onion, garlic and jalapeños in olive oil until lightly browned, 4 to 5 minutes. Stir in chicken, chicken broth, lime juice, tomato, salt and pepper. Gently simmer until chicken is cooked, about 25 minutes. Stir in avocado and cilantro and heat through. Adjust seasoning to taste. Ladle soup into bowl and top with baked tortilla strips.

Makes 2 to 3 servings.

Chilled Cucumber Cilantro Soup

1 c buttermilk
2 cucumbers, peeled, seeded and chopped
1 ripe avocado
1/4 c chicken broth (can substitute vegetable broth for vegetarian)
1 Tbl fresh cilantro, chopped
2 Tbl fresh lemon juice
1/4 tsp ground cumin

In a large measuring cup combine buttermilk plus ice cubes to measure 1 1/2 c total. In a blender, blend buttermilk mixture with the avocado, broth, cilantro, lemon juice, cumin, and half the cucumbers until smooth. Divide into chilled bowls and stir remaining cucumbers into each serving.

Makes 3 to 4 servings.

Avocado Soup with Green Peppercorn

1 medium white onion, diced
1Tbl ground coriander
1 Tbl olive oil
4 large ripe avocados, peeled, pitted and coarsely chopped
1/3 c green peppercorns in brine, drained
Salt and freshly ground black pepper to taste
2 cloves garlic, minced
1 tsp cumin
21/2 qt light chicken stock
Fresh cilantro and peppercorns to garnish

In a large saucepan, cook onion, garlic and spices in olive oil over medium/high heat for about 10 minutes, stirring frequently. Add avocados and chicken stock, bring to a boil and then reduce heat to medium/low. Cook 20 minutes. Cool to room temperature.
Puree soup in blender until smooth.
Return to saucepan and bring back to a boil over medium/high heat. Add peppercorn, then reduce to medium/low heat and simmer for about 10 minutes.
Serve immediately. Garnish with fresh cilantro and peppercorns.

Makes 4 servings.

Avocado Shrimp Soup

1 small red onion, diced
4 c chicken broth
4 sprigs parsley
1/8 c chives, chopped
2 medium ripe avocados, peeled, pitted and coarsely chopped
1/2 c cooked small shrimp, shelled and deveined
2 stalks celery, finely chopped
1 bay leaf
1 c low-fat sour cream
Salt and freshly ground black pepper to taste

Place onion, celery, broth, bay leaf, parsley, salt and black pepper in a large saucepan and bring to boil over medium/high heat. Reduce heat and simmer over medium/low heat for 15 minutes. Strain and reserve stock. Place avocados in blender or food processor; puree avocados while slowly adding stock. When mixture is smooth, return to saucepan and heat gently. Add shrimp and cook over low heat until thoroughly heated. Do not boil. Serve with a dollop of sour cream in each serving sprinkled lightly with chives.

Makes 4 to 6 servings.

Avocado Gazpacho Soup

2 large cucumbers
3 c chicken broth (can substitute vegetable broth for vegetarian)
1 tsp hot pepper sauce (or more to taste)
1/4 c firmly packed fresh cilantro, chopped
1 Tbl fresh lime juice
2 ripe avocados, peeled, pitted and coarsely chopped
Salt to taste
6 green onions, chopped finely
Garlic croutons
Cilantro sprigs

Cut one cucumber into chunks and process with 2 cups of broth, cilantro, lime juice, salt and hot pepper sauce. Pit, peel and process avocados with pureed mixture and add the third cup of broth. Process briefly to coarsely puree the avocado, leaving some chunks. Chill at least 2 hours.

Just before serving, dice the green onions and peel, seed and chop the second cucumber. Pour soup into bowls and garnish each one with fresh croutons and fresh cilantro sprigs.

Set out minced onion and diced cucumber to add individually.

Makes about 6 servings.

Avocado Curry Soup

2 avocados, peeled, pitted and cubed
2 1/2 c chicken stock
1 Tbl fresh parsley, chopped
1 tsp curry powder
Salt and white pepper to taste
1/2 c whipping cream

Blend avocados in food processor or blender with 1 cup of chicken stock until smooth. Stir in the remaining stock and the other ingredients and blend until smooth. Chill for at least 1/2 hour before serving.
Garnish with sliced avocados.

Makes 4 servings.

Avocado Soup with Radishes and Cilantro Cream

2 Tbl avocado oil
3 Tbl olive oil
1 medium yellow onion, chopped
4 cloves garlic, minced
1 (1 1/2 in) piece ginger, peeled
and minced
3 Serrano peppers, stemmed,
seeded and minced
4 c chicken stock

Heat avocado oil in a medium saucepan over medium/high heat and add chopped onion. Sauté for 5 minutes, then add garlic, ginger and 2 of the peppers. Sauté for another 5 minutes. Add stock and simmer for 10 minutes. While vegetables and stock simmer, peel and pit avocados. Chop avocados and toss them in the juice of 1 lime. Place half the avocados in the blender. Add stock and vegetable mixture to blender and puree until smooth.
Chill for 2 hours.
To make cilantro cream, mix sour cream and half and half together. Add chopped cilantro, the remaining chili pepper, ground coriander and salt to taste. Chill until ready to use.
Cut radishes in small julienne and toss with olive oil, the juice of half a lime and salt to taste. Chill until ready to use.
Taste chilled soup and add salt and lime to taste. Ladle into chilled soup bowls. Top each serving with a tablespoon of cilantro cream and a tablespoon of julienned radishes.

Makes 4 to 6 servings.

Spicy Zucchini Noodle Soup with Avocado Salsa

Salsa Ingredients
1 tsp cumin seeds, toasted
1 medium ripe-firm avocado, peeled, pitted and diced
2 Tbl fresh lemon juice
2 medium tomatoes, diced
3 green onions, thinly sliced
1 medium garlic clove, minced
1/8 tsp cayenne pepper
1 Tbl fresh cilantro, chopped

Soup Ingredients
2 Tbl extra-virgin olive oil
3 medium cloves garlic, minced
1/2 tsp chili powder
1 tsp ground cumin
1 large red onion, chopped coarsely
2 medium zucchini, diced
1 small red bell pepper, cored and diced
1/4 c diced tomatoes
1/4 c fresh cilantro, chopped finely
2 c water
1 c plain low-fat yogurt
1/2 c Parmesan cheese, finely grated
12oz dried whole-wheat ribbon pasta

Make salsa an hour before serving time to allow flavors to blend. Toast cumin seeds on cookie sheet in preheated 400 degree F oven for about 5 to 7 minutes. Mix all salsa ingredients in a small bowl, cover and refrigerate.

Boil pasta in a separate pan until tender, drain and rinse with cold water. Set aside for later.

Combine all ingredients for soup except yogurt, Parmesan cheese and pasta in a large saucepan. Heat over medium/high heat to a boil and cook for about 15 minutes. Stir in yogurt and cooked pasta and remove from heat. Serve sprinkled with Parmesan cheese and topped with salsa. Makes 6 servings.

Avocado Cilantro Soup

8 medium green onions
1/2 c fresh cilantro
2 large cloves garlic, chopped
1 medium, ripe avocado, peeled, pitted and sliced
1 1/2 c plain nonfat yogurt
1/2 c skim buttermilk
2 Tbl lime juice
1/2 tsp curry powder
1/8 tsp ground red pepper

In a food processor, combine green onions, cilantro and garlic; process until finely chopped. Add avocado; process until smooth. Add yogurt, buttermilk. 1/4 cup water, lime juice, curry powder and red pepper to food processor; process until smooth. Cover and refrigerate at least 1 hour, until well chilled.
Serves about 4.

Spicy Avocado Soup

1 small cucumber, seeded and sliced
1 (7oz) can corn kernels, drained
1 tomato, chopped
1 jalapeños, seeded and minced
1 Serrano pepper, chopped finely
2 Tbl fresh cilantro, chopped
1/8 tsp ground cumin
2 Tbl fresh lemon juice
2 ripe avocados, peeled, pitted and chunked
1 1/2 c milk
1 c chicken broth (can substitute vegetable broth for vegetarian)

In a large bowl combine cucumber, corn, tomato, jalapeño and Serrano pepper. In food processor, process avocados, milk and broth until smooth. Pour into bowl. Combine with cucumber mixture and mix well. Mix in cilantro, cumin and lemon juice. Press plastic wrap against top of soup; chill at least 2 hours. Soup will discolor upon exposure to air.

Makes 3 servings.

There are seven varieties of avocados grown commercially in California, Haas being the most popular. They are as follows:

- Bacon is a mid-winter green variety, available late fall into early spring. It is oval shaped, with smooth, thin green skin, a medium- to large-seed and a light taste.
- Fuerte is harvested late fall through spring. It is pear-shaped with thin, smooth green skin, a medium seed and pale green flesh.
- Gwen is a Haas-like green variety, but slightly larger. It has pebbly-thick green skin, a small- to medium-seed and creamy, gold-green flesh. Green skin turns dull when ripe.
- Haas is distinctive with green skin that becomes purplish-black when it becomes ripe. It has pebbly-thick, but pliant skin, a small- to medium-seed and pale green flesh with a creamy texture.
- Pinkerton avocados have small seeds and yield more fruit per tree. They are a long pear-shaped fruit, with medium-thick green skin with slight pebbling and creamy pale green flesh. Its green skin deepens in color as it ripens.
- Reed is a large round fruit available in the summer months and early fall. It has thick, green skin with slight pebbling, a medium seed and buttery flesh. Skin remains green when ripened.
- Zutano is recognized for its shiny, yellow-green skin. It is one of the first varieties harvested when the season begins in September and is available through early winter. It is pear-shaped with an average to large size. Its flesh is pale green with a light texture. Its skin retains yellow-green color when ripened.

Side Dishes

Cottage Cheese Avocado Salsa

1 ear corn, husked and cleaned
1 (15oz) can black beans
1 (32oz) container low-fat cottage cheese
1 ripe avocado, peeled, pitted and diced
2 plum tomatoes, seeded and diced
2 Tbl fresh lime juice
1/4 c red onion, chopped
3 Tbl extra-virgin olive oil
3 Tbl fresh cilantro, chopped
2 jalapeños, minced
Salt and freshly ground black pepper to taste.

Boil corn on the cob in a medium saucepan over medium/high heat until tender, about 15 minutes. Cool under running water and slice kernels from cob. Set aside.
Cook the black beans in a small saucepan over medium heat until warm and tender, about 10 minutes. Strain and rinse under cold water. Set aside.
Place cottage cheese in a serving bowl. Add avocados, tomatoes, black beans, corn, lime juice, red onion, olive oil, cilantro and jalapeños. Season to taste with salt and black pepper. Mix well, cover and refrigerate until ready to serve.

Makes 3 to 4 cups.

SIDES

Habanero Mango Salsa

1 ripe avocado, peeled, pitted and diced
1 lime, juiced
1 mango, peeled, seeded and diced
1 small red onion, chopped
1 Habanero pepper, seeded and chopped
1 Tbl fresh cilantro, chopped
1/2 tsp chili powder
Salt and freshly ground black pepper to taste

Mix diced avocado and lime juice in a medium bowl. Add mango, onion, Habanero pepper, cilantro, chili powder and mix thoroughly. Salt and pepper to taste. Serve at room temperature. Makes about 2 cups.

Black Bean and Papaya Salsa

1 c black beans, cooked and drained
2 ripe papayas, peeled, seeded and diced into small squares
1/2 red bell pepper, deveined and diced into small squares
1/2 green bell pepper, deveined and diced into small squares
1/2 red onion, diced into small squares
1 large ripe-firm avocado, peeled, pitted and diced
3/4 c pineapple juice
1/2 c fresh lime juice
1/2 cup fresh cilantro, chopped
2 Tbl ground cumin
1 Tbl Serrano chili, minced
Salt
Fresh cracked black pepper

In a large mixing bowl, combine all ingredients and mix together well. Serve chilled or at room temperature.

Makes about 2 cups.

Avocado Salsa

1 avocado, peeled, pitted and diced
4 small red tomatoes, diced
1 small red onion, diced
1 green pepper, seeded and diced
1 jalapeño, finely diced
1 green chili, finely diced
1 garlic clove, minced
Salt to taste
2 Tbl red wine vinegar
1 Tbl extra-virgin olive oil
4 drops Tabasco sauce

Combine avocado, tomatoes, onion, jalapeño and green chili and mix well. Mash garlic and salt in a small bowl. Add vinegar, oil and Tabasco sauce. Pour this mixture over avocado, tomatoes, onion, jalapeño and green chili and toss. Serve chilled or at room temperature.

Makes 2 to 3 cups.

Avocado and Roasted Tomatillo Salsa

1/2 lb tomatillos, roasted
1 red onion, halved
2 cloves garlic
2 Tbl fresh cilantro, chopped
1 tsp salt
1 jalapeño, seeded and chopped finely
2 small/medium avocados, peeled, pitted and chopped
2 Tbl fresh lime juice

Preheat broiler. Remove husks and rinse tomatillos under warm water to remove stickiness. Halve onion and arrange on rack of broiler with tomatillos and garlic. Broil vegetables about 8 minutes, turning once, until softened and lightly charred.
Peel garlic and place in food processor with tomatillos, 1 onion half, cilantro and salt. Remove seeds from jalapeño and chop finely. Add jalapeño to tomatillo mixture and puree until mixture is almost smooth. Transfer to a bowl.
In a smaller bowl, coat avocados in lime juice and mix well. Add avocados to tomatillo mixture, chill for 30 minutes and serve.

Makes about 11/2 cup.

SIDES

Corn and Black Olive Salsa

1 1/2 c corn
2 (2 1/4 oz) cans sliced ripe olives, drained
1 red bell pepper, deveined and chopped
1 red onion, chopped
4 garlic cloves, chopped finely
1/3 c olive oil
1/4 c fresh lemon juice
3 Tbl cider vinegar
1 tsp dried oregano
4 ripe avocados
Salt and pepper to taste

Combine corn, olives, red pepper and onion in a large bowl. In a small bowl combine garlic, oil, lemon juice, vinegar, oregano and salt and pepper to taste. Pour garlic mixture into corn mixture and mix well. Cover and refrigerate overnight. Just before serving add chopped avocados and stir into salsa.

Makes about 3 cups.

Avocado Orange Salsa

3/4 c orange segments
3/4 c avocado, peeled, pitted and cut into 1/2 inch cubes
2 limes, juiced
1/4 c red onion, diced finely
1/4 c fresh cilantro, chopped finely
1 pinch dried red pepper flakes
Salt and ground black pepper to taste

Combine all ingredients and toss gently.
Refrigerate until ready to serve.

Makes about 11/2 cups.

SIDES

Avocado Feta Cheese Salsa

2 plum tomatoes, chopped
1 ripe avocado, peeled, pitted and chopped
1/4 c red onion, chopped finely
1 clove garlic, minced
1 Tbl fresh parsley, chopped
1 Tbl olive oil
1 Tbl red wine vinegar
4 oz crumbled feta cheese
Freshly ground black pepper to taste

In a bowl, gently stir together tomatoes, avocados, onion and garlic. Mix in parsley and oregano. Gently stir in olive oil and vinegar. Then stir in feta. Season to taste with freshly ground black pepper. Cover and chill for 2 to 6 hours.

Makes about 11/2 cups.

Mango Papaya Salsa

1 mango, peeled, seeded and diced
1 papaya, peeled, seeded and diced
1 large red bell pepper, seeded, deveined and diced
1 ripe avocado, peeled, pitted and diced
1/2 red onion, peeled and diced
2 Tbl fresh cilantro, chopped
2 Tbl balsamic vinegar
Salt and pepper to taste

In a medium bowl, mix mango, papaya, red bell pepper, avocado, red onion, cilantro and balsamic vinegar. Season to taste with salt and pepper. Cover and chill in refrigerator at least 30 minutes prior to serving.

Makes about 2 to 3 cups.

SIDES

Jalapeño Mango Salsa

1 mango, peeled, seeded and diced
1 avocado, peeled, pitted and diced
4 medium tomatoes, diced
2 jalapeño peppers, minced
1/2 c fresh cilantro, chopped
3 cloves garlic, minced
1 tsp salt
2 Tbl fresh lime juice
1/2 c red onion, chopped
3 Tbl olive oil
Black pepper to taste

In a medium bowl, combine mango, avocado, tomatoes, jalapeños, cilantro and garlic. Stir in the salt, lime juice, red onion and olive oil. Black pepper to taste. Chill in a covered container for at least 30 minutes prior to serving. Makes about 3 cups.

Roasted Corn Guacamole

4 ripe avocados, peeled, pitted and mashed
1 c roasted corn kernels
1/4 c fresh lime juice
1 medium red Roma tomato, seeded and diced
4 cloves garlic, chopped finely
3 jalapeño peppers, chopped finely with seeds
1 tsp ground cumin
Salt and freshly ground black pepper to taste

In a medium bowl, coarsely mash avocados. Fold in remaining ingredients. Squeeze lime juice into avocado mixture and serve.

Makes about 2 cups.

SIDES

Serrano Mango Guacamole

2 ripe avocados, peeled, pitted and coarsely mashed
1 ripe mango, chopped
1/2 red onion, chopped
1 medium red tomato, seeded and diced
1 clove garlic, minced
2 Serrano chilies, seeded and chopped
2 Tbl fresh cilantro, chopped
2 Tbl fresh lime juice
1 Tbl low fat sour cream
Salt and freshly ground black pepper to taste

Combine all ingredients and chill at least 1 hour to let flavors mix.

Makes about 2 cups.

Blackened Tomatillo Guacamole

12 medium tomatillos, husked and rinsed
1/2 c white onion, chopped finely
1/2 c red onion, chopped finely
1/2 c fresh cilantro, chopped coarsely
4 Serrano chilies, seeded and minced
2 Tbl fresh lime juice
3 large ripe avocados, peeled, pitted and coarsely mashed
Salt and freshly ground black pepper to taste

Preheat broiler. Line rimmed baking sheet with aluminum foil. Place tomatillos on prepared baking sheet. Broil until tomatillos are just blackened in spots and tender, about 8 minutes each side. Combine onions, cilantro, chilies and lime juice in large bowl. Add roasted tomatillos and any juices from baking sheet to onion mixture. Using fork mash coarsely. Add avocados and mash with fork until mixture is very coarsely pureed and some chunks remain. Season to taste with salt and freshly ground black pepper. Makes 3 to 4 cups.

SIDES

Mint and White Onion Guacamole

4 ripe avocados, peeled, pitted and mashed
2 Tbl fresh lemon juice
1 Tbl honey
1 large plum tomato, diced finely
1/2 c white onion, chopped finely
1/2 c fresh cilantro, chopped finely
1/4 c fresh mint, chopped finely
3 Tbl Serrano peppers, chopped finely

Salt and freshly ground black pepper to taste.
In a medium/large bowl, coarsely mash avocados. Stir in lemon juice and honey.
Fold in remaining ingredients. Serve immediately.

Makes about 3 cups.

Spicy Fruit Guacamole

1/3 c white onions, chopped finely
3 Serrano chilies, chopped finely
1 tsp coarse salt
4 large ripe avocados, peeled, pitted and coarsely mashed
3 Tbl fresh lime juice
3/4 c pear, peeled and diced finely
3/4 c seedless grapes, halved
3/4 c pomegranate seeds
2 Tbl honey
Freshly ground black pepper to taste

Process onions, chilies and salt into a rough paste. Gradually add avocado, coarsely mashing it, leaving chunks. Stir in the lemon juice. In a separate bowl mix the pear, grapes and 1/2 cup of pomegranate seeds with honey and black pepper to taste. Combine fruits with avocados mix and then sprinkle remaining pomegranate seeds over guacamole. Chill until ready to serve.

Makes about 3 cups.

SIDES

Cranberry Guacamole

2 ripe avocados, peeled, pitted and coarsely mashed
1 (7oz) can salsa verde
3 Tbl fresh cilantro, chopped coarsely
1 Tbl fresh lemon juice
1 Tbl fresh orange juice
3 tsp jalapeño peppers, chopped finely
1 tsp coarse garlic salt
1/2 c dried cranberries
1 Tbl white onion, finely chopped
White pepper to taste

In a medium bowl, coarsely mash avocados and add salsa verde, cilantro, lemon juice, orange juice, jalapeño and garlic salt. Mix well. Fold in cranberries and onion. Season to taste with white pepper.
Serve with tortilla chips or sliced vegetables.

Makes about 2 cups.

Roasted Poblano Chili Salsa

7 ripe avocados, peeled, pitted and coarsely mashed
1/2 c fresh cilantro, chopped coarsely
1/2 c tomato, chopped
1/2 c red onion, chopped
2 Tbl fresh lime juice
1 tsp cumin
1 tsp chili powder
2 roasted Poblano chilies, chopped
1 Tbl garlic, minced
Salt and freshly ground black pepper to taste

Heat broiler. Slice Poblano chilies in half and place in broiler for about 2 to 3 minutes, until lightly browned. Remove and chop.
In a large mixing bowl, coarsely mash avocados, leaving some chunks. Add remaining ingredients into avocado bowl and mix. Season to taste with salt and pepper.
Serve immediately with tortilla chips.

Makes about 3 to 4 cups.

SIDES

Vegetarian Ceviche With Lime

2 lb extra firm tofu
2 Tbl vegetarian Worcestershire sauce
4 large tomatoes, seeded and chopped
1/2 c freshly squeezed lime juice
1 c fresh cilantro, chopped
1 small jalapeño, seeded and minced
Salt to taste
1 small red onion, finely chopped
1 medium green pepper, finely chopped
2 Tbl fresh ginger root, peeled and minced
2 cloves garlic, minced
1 c canned coconut milk
2 large avocados, peeled, seeded and chopped

Preheat oven to 400 degrees F. Drain the tofu and cut into 1-inch cubes. Pat dry with a paper towel. Mix tofu with Worcestershire sauce. Spread tofu out evenly on a parchment-lined cookie sheet and bake for 30 minutes, turning tofu over once in the middle of baking. Cool to room temperature. When tofu has cooled, mix together all remaining ingredients in a large bowl. Add the tofu cubes and toss gently. Allow the flavors to blend in the refrigerator for at least 2 hours to overnight before serving.

Makes 4 to 5 cups.

Salsa Fresca Guacamole

2c plum tomatoes, chopped finely
1 c white onion, chopped finely
1/4 c fresh cilantro, chopped coarsely
3 Ancho chilies, deveined, seeded and chopped
1 clove garlic, minced
2 limes, juiced
1/2 c vegetable broth
Salt and pepper to taste

4 ripe avocados, peeled, pitted and coarsely mashed
2 limes, juiced
Salt and pepper to taste

To make red salsa fresca, mix chopped onion, cilantro, chilies, garlic, lime juice and vegetable broth in a medium bowl. Season to taste with salt and ground black pepper and mix well.

In another bowl, coarsely mash avocados with lime juice and then salt and pepper to taste.

Mix salsa fresca with mashed avocados. Serve immediately with fresh tortilla chips. Makes about 3 to 4 cups.

SIDES

Cherry Tomato Guacamole

2 large avocados, peeled, pitted and coarsely ground
2Tbl fresh lemon juice
1/2 c red bell pepper, diced finely
1/2 c cherry tomatoes, halved
1/4 c green onions, sliced thinly
1/2 red onion, chopped finely
3 cloves garlic, chopped finely
1/2 tsp fresh thyme, chopped
1/2 tsp salt
1/4 tsp freshly ground black pepper
1/4 tsp cayenne pepper
1 Tbl fresh cilantro, chopped

Coarsely mash avocados, leaving chunks and then stir in lemon juice. Fold in remaining ingredients.
Serve immediately.

Makes about 2 to 3 cups.

Anaheim Asparagus Guacamole

1 medium Anaheim chili
1 tsp extra-virgin olive oil
5 fresh asparagus spears, ends trimmed
1/2 c nonfat plain yogurt
2 medium avocados, peeled, pitted and cubed
1 plum tomato, seeded and diced
1 Tbl green onion, chopped
1/4 c fresh cilantro, chopped
1 Tbl fresh lime juice
Dash of garlic powder
1/2 tsp salt
1/2 tsp freshly ground black pepper

Preheat broiler. Wearing rubber gloves to protect skin, rub chili with oil and broil for 5 minutes. Turn chili with tongs so all sides are equally charred. Transfer chili to a plastic bag, seal and let steam for about 10 minutes or until skin is loosened. Remove stem, skin and seeds from chili and dice. Set aside.

Fill medium sauté pan halfway with water and bring to a boil. Prepare a medium-sized bowl of ice water. Place asparagus spears into boiling water for 3 to 4 minutes or until just tender. Remove and plunge spears into icy water to halt cooking and preserve color. When cool, remove, dry thoroughly and chop into 1-inch pieces. Transfer to blender or food processor, add yogurt and avocado and process until smooth.

Transfer to a mixing bowl and stir in remaining ingredients. Serve with fresh tortilla chips.

Makes about 3 cups.

SIDES

Citrus Guacamole

3 ripe avocados, peeled, pitted and coarsely mashed
3 tomatoes, peeled, seeded and diced
1/4 c red onion, minced
1 lime, juiced and grated rind
2 Tbl fresh lemon juice
2 Tbl fresh orange juice
1/2 tsp coarse salt
1/4 c low-fat mayonnaise
1/4 c low-fat sour cream
3 dashes hot pepper sauce

Combine all ingredients and serve immediately with tortilla chips.

Makes about 3 cups.

Green Chili Tofu Guacamole

4 ripe avocados, peeled, pitted and mashed coarsely
1 (10 1/2 oz) pack of tofu, drained
1/4 red onion, chopped
1 1/2 Tbl plain yogurt
2 cloves garlic, pressed
1 tsp Tabasco sauce
1 tsp salt
Garnish with sliced red bell pepper

Drain excess water from tofu and combine with plain yogurt in a small bowl. Mash with a fork. In a large bowl, coarsely mash avocados, leaving chunks. Mix tofu and yogurt with avocados and add pressed garlic, Tabasco sauce and salt. Mix well and garnish with thinly sliced red bell pepper.
Serve with tortilla chips or fresh vegetables.

Makes about 4 cups.

Sweet Onion Guacamole

4 ripe avocados, peeled, pitted and coarsely mashed
4 Tbl low-fat plain yogurt
1/2 c red onion, chopped finely
1/2 c yellow onion, chopped finely
4 cloves garlic, minced
4 Tbl fresh cilantro, chopped finely
1 Chile de Arbol, dried and finely crushed
1 tsp cumin powder
1/2 tsp salt
1/2 tsp pepper
2 Tbl fresh lime juice

In a medium bowl, coarsely mash avocados, leaving chunks. Combine all remaining ingredients, cover and refrigerate for about 1 hour before serving.
Serve with tortilla chips.

Makes about 4 cups.

Green Salsa Guacamole

2 ripe avocados, peeled, pitted and coarsely mashed
1/4 c salsa verde
1 1/4 tsp grated lemon peel
1 Tbl fresh lemon juice
1 tsp coarse garlic salt
3 Tbl red bell pepper, chopped finely
3 Tbl fresh basil leaves, chopped
1 medium shallot, chopped finely

In a medium bowl, combine avocados, salsa, lemon peel and juice and garlic salt. Stir in bell pepper, basil and shallot.
Serve with tortilla chips or fresh vegetables.

Makes about 2 to 3 cups.

Black Bean Pepper Guacamole

2 ripe avocados, peeled, pitted and coarsely mashed
1 Tbl fresh lemon juice
2 cloves garlic, chopped finely
1/2 tsp salt
1/2 c black beans, rinsed and drained
3Tbl red onion, chopped
3 Tbl tomato, chopped
2 pickled jalapeños, chopped
Freshly ground black pepper to taste.

In a medium bowl combine avocados, lemon juice, garlic and salt. Stir in beans, onion, tomato and jalapeño. Season to taste with freshly ground black pepper. Serve with fresh tortilla chips.

Makes about 3 cups.

Basic Guacamole

2 ripe avocados, peeled, pitted and coarsely mashed
1 large ripe tomato, diced
1/4 c red onion, finely chopped
2 cloves garlic, minced
3 Tbl fresh cilantro, chopped finely
1 large lime, juiced
1/2 tsp ground cumin
Salt and freshly ground black pepper to taste

Coarsely mash avocados, leaving some chunks and add all remaining ingredients and mix well. Serve immediately with fresh tortilla chips.

Makes about 3 cups.

SIDES

Garbanzo Guacamole

1 can Garbanzo beans, drained and rinsed
1 Tbl fresh lemon juice
1 clove garlic, crushed
1 medium red onion, chopped
1 ripe avocado, peeled, pitted and chopped
1 medium red tomato, chopped
4 green onions, thinly sliced
1 Tbl green chilies, chopped

Place garbanzo beans in a food processor or blender. Add lemon juice and garlic and process until garbanzos are slightly chopped, about 30 seconds. Add onion and avocado and mix again, leaving mixture chunky. Place mixture in a bowl and add remaining ingredients. Mix well, cover and chill for 1 hour before serving. Makes about 2 cups.

California Cuisine, Light and Flavorful

Avocados embody the soul of the California cuisine, light yet filled with flavor. They can deliciously fit the bill of accent piece to a meal, or the main course with their smooth, fruity flavor. In addition to their delectable taste and versatility, these fruits are well known for their nutritional value.

Avocados pack a healthy punch as a rich source of mono unsaturated fatty acids, which have been shown to offer significant protection against breast cancer and to lower cholesterol levels. They are also a good source of potassium, a mineral that regulates blood pressure. Potassium helps guard against heart disease, high blood pressure or stroke. They are also a great source of folate, a nutrient important for heart health. Avocados contain the highest amount of carotenoid lutein of all commonly eaten fruits. Carotenoids are lipid (fat) soluble; so the fat in avocados is a necessity nature saw fit to incorporate so these bioactive carotenoids could be easily dissolved into the blood stream. Mixing avocados into a fresh salad or adding some chopped avocado to your fresh salsa will increase your body's ability to absorb the health-promoting carotenoids that vegetables provide.

In addition to soups, salads, dips, breads and iced desserts, the avocado has found increasing use as a cooking oil. Due to its high mono unsaturated fat content, the avocado as a refined cooking oil has some excellent health benefits.

- It is very light and mixes well with other foods.
- Its mild, delicate flavor enhances the flavors of other foods, rather than dominating them.
- Avocado oil has a higher smoke point (about 490 degrees F), which is the point in which the oil begins to break down, than many other oils.

Sandwiches

Avocado Sandwich

8 slices ripe avocado
1/4 c Italian salad dressing
1 Tbl light mayonnaise
4 slices whole-wheat bread, toasted
4 slices low-fat cheddar cheese
8 thin tomato slices
1 c alfalfa sprouts
Salt and freshly ground black pepper to taste

Toss avocado slices gently with Italian dressing; drain well and reserve dressing. Spread mayonnaise evenly over 1 side of each bread slice. Top bread slices evenly with avocado, cheese, tomato and alfalfa sprouts.

Drizzle open sandwiches with Italian dressing, season to taste then close and serve immediately.

Makes 2 sandwiches.

SANDWICHES

Spicy Avocado Sandwich

2 Focaccia rolls, toasted
1 medium ripe avocado, peeled, pitted and thinly sliced
1 medium Roma tomato, thinly sliced
2 green onions, thinly sliced
1 Tbl Dijon mustard

Preheat broiler.
Place focaccia rolls, sliced open, in preheated broiler until lightly toasted, about 1 to 2 minutes.
Slice avocado, tomato and green onion lengthwise. Spread Dijon mustard evenly on rolls. Layer avocado, tomato and green onion, fold and slice at an angle.

Makes 2 sandwiches.

Avocado Eggplant Sandwich

8 slices whole-wheat bread
1/2 yellow bell pepper, seeded and thinly sliced
1/2 red bell pepper, seeded and thinly sliced
1 large eggplant
1 large ripe avocado, peeled, pitted and thinly sliced
1 tomato, thinly sliced
1/2 red onion, thinly sliced
4 jalapeños, seeded and thinly sliced
Shredded lettuce
Dash of red chili powder
Salt and freshly ground black pepper to taste

Thinly slice eggplant and grill in skillet over medium heat, with olive oil, red chili powder and salt until lightly browned. Lightly toast bread, then layer yellow and red bell peppers, grilled eggplant, avocado, tomato, red onion, jalapeños and lettuce. Salt and pepper to taste, fold and slice diagonally.
Serve immediately.

Makes 4 sandwiches.

SANDWICHES

Vegan Avocado Delight Sandwich

2 slices vegan or whole-wheat bread
1 large ripe avocado, peeled, pitted and sliced thinly
Dash of salt
2 Tbl vegan mayonnaise
1/4 c bean sprouts
2 slices tomato
1 slice tofu or vegan cheese
4 Tbl sunflower seeds

Spread mayonnaise on bread evenly and sprinkle sunflower seeds over top. Layer with lightly salted avocado slices, tomato, cheese and sprouts.
Slice sandwich diagonally and serve immediately.

Makes 1 sandwich.

Avocado Pita

1 large ripe avocado, peeled, pitted and chopped
1 large plum tomato, chopped
1/2 small white onion, chopped
1 clove garlic, chopped
1 Tbl olive oil
1/4 c cooked black beans
1 pita bread

Chop avocado, tomato, white onion and garlic clove. Put chopped garlic through a garlic press. Mix all vegetables with olive oil. Rinse beans well and combine all ingredients in a medium bowl.
Stuff pita and serve immediately.

Makes 1 pita.

SANDWICHES

Vegan Avocado and Cream Cheese Pita

1 Tbl vegan cream cheese
1/2 ripe avocado, peeled, pitted and coarsely mashed
1 Tbl sunflower seeds
1/4 c spinach, rinsed and stemmed
2 slices tomato
1 pita, sliced in half

Smear one side of the pita with vegan cream cheese and the other side with mashed avocado. Sprinkle with sunflower seeds and then add lettuce and sliced tomato. Fold and serve immediately.

Makes 1 pita sandwich.

Avocado and Sprout Sandwich

4 slices whole-wheat bread, lightly toasted
1 Tbl low-fat ranch dressing
1 ripe avocado, peeled, pitted and thinly sliced
1/2 c alfalfa sprouts
2 lettuce leaves
2 large slices tomato

Lightly toast bread. Evenly spread ranch dressing over 1 side of each slice of bread. Top with avocado slices, alfalfa sprouts, lettuce and tomatoes. Close sandwiches, slice diagonally and serve immediately.

Makes 2 sandwiches.

SANDWICHES

Avocado, Olive and Tomato Sandwiches

2 whole-wheat rolls, lightly toasted
1 c green olives
2 Tbl extra-virgin olive oil
1 Tsp garlic, chopped
1 small ripe tomato, sliced thinly
1 large ripe avocado, peeled, pitted and thinly sliced

Slice rolls lengthwise and lightly toast in broiler, about 1 minute.
Place olives, olive oil and garlic in blender or food processor and mix until paste forms. Spread paste onto toasted rolls and top with tomato and avocado slices. Fold and serve immediately.

Makes 2 sandwiches.

Avocado, Tomato and Onion Sandwich

2 whole-wheat rolls
2 Tbl olive oil
1/2 Tbl garlic powder
1/4 Tbl basil
1/4 tsp oregano
Dash of salt
Dash of black pepper
1 Roma tomato, sliced
1/2 red onion, thinly sliced
1 large ripe avocado, peeled, pitted and sliced

Preheat oven to 375 degrees F. In a small bowl mix olive oil, garlic powder, basil, oregano, salt and pepper to make olive oil sauce.

Slice rolls lengthwise. Layer bottom of each roll with tomato, onion and avocado. Drizzle olive oil sauce over top of vegetables and over top slices of bread.

Place cookie sheet in center oven rack and bake open-faced sandwiches 10 to 12 minutes, or until lightly toasted.

Serve warm.

Makes 2 sandwiches.

SANDWICHES

Red Cabbage Avocado Sandwiches

1 whole-wheat roll, lightly toasted
1 Tbl low-fat cream cheese
1 tsp chives, thinly sliced
1 medium ripe avocado, peeled, pitted and thinly sliced
1 lettuce leaf
1 red cabbage leaf
1/2 cucumber, peeled and sliced
2 thin slices tomato

Lightly toast roll in broiler, about 1 minute. In a small bowl, mix cream cheese and chives. Spread cream cheese mix evenly over both sides of the roll. Layer sliced avocado and add lettuce, cabbage, cucumber slices and tomato slices. Fold, slice sandwich diagonally and serve.

Makes 1 sandwich.

Avocado and Cucumber Sandwich

1 whole-wheat roll
1 ripe avocado, peeled, pitted and thinly sliced
Salt and pepper to taste
2 slices tomato
5 slices peeled cucumber
1 Tbl extra-virgin olive oil
1/2 small lemon
Thinly sliced low-fat cheddar cheese
1/2 c alfalfa sprouts

Preheat oven to 350 degrees F. Pour olive oil into small bowl and squeeze 1/2 lemon into bowl. Place sliced avocados into olive oil/lemon juice bowl and mix. Salt and pepper to taste avocado slices.
Slice roll diagonally and place marinated avocado slices into roll. Top with tomato, cucumber and cheese. Place open sandwich on a cookie sheet in center rack in oven. Bake about 10 minutes or until sandwich is warmed and lightly toasted. Add sprouts, fold and serve immediately.

Makes 1 sandwich.

SANDWICHES

Avocado, Hummus and Tomato Sandwich

2 slices whole-wheat bread
1/4 c hummus, garlic flavored
1/2 ripe avocado, peeled, pitted and thinly sliced
1 lemon wedge
2 slices Roma tomato
Salt and freshly ground black pepper to taste

Spread 1 side of both bread slices liberally with humus. Layer bread with sliced avocado and squeeze lemon juice over the top. Layer top with tomatoes and then salt and freshly ground black pepper to taste.
Serve immediately.

Makes 1 sandwich.

Sun Dried Tomato and Avocado Sandwich

2 slices whole-wheat bread, lightly toasted
1 heaping Tbl sun dried tomatoes
1/2 ripe avocado, peeled, pitted and sliced thinly
1 thin slice low-fat sharp cheddar cheese
1/4 c alfalfa sprouts

Lightly toast bread. While bread is toasting, place sun dried tomatoes on microwave-safe plate and microwave on high for 30 seconds. When done, drain oil and pat dry. Layer sun dried tomatoes, avocado slices, cheddar cheese and alfalfa sprouts on toasted bread. Close sandwich and slice diagonally.
Serve immediately.

Makes 1 sandwich.

SANDWICHES

Avocado Mushroom Sandwich

2 slices multi-grain bread
1/2 ripe avocado, peeled, pitted and thinly sliced
1/4 c fresh mushrooms, thinly sliced
2 slices ripe tomato
2 slices low-fat or vegan cheddar cheese

Preheat oven to 400 degrees F. Place bread slices on cookie sheet and layer one side with avocado, mushrooms and tomato slices and top with cheese slices. Place cookie sheet in oven and bake about 5 to 7 minutes, just until cheese melts.
Serve immediately.

Makes 1 sandwich.

Avocado Salad Flatbread Sandwich

3/4 c white wine vinegar, divided
1/2 Tbl fresh garlic, chopped finely
Salt and freshly ground black pepper to taste
1 c olive oil
2 c sweet onion, chopped
2 c tomato, chopped
Flat bread, such as pita, 24 rounds, about 7-in in diameter
Hearts of Romaine leaves, as needed
12 oz shaved Romano cheese
6 lbs California avocados
Jack or Fontina cheese in 1 oz slices may be substituted

To make vinaigrette, whisk together 1/2 c vinegar, garlic, salt and pepper. Whisk in oil; reserve.

Combine onion, tomato and remaining 1/4 c vinegar; reserve.

Just before serving, dice avocado and fold into onion and tomato mixture.

Brush one round of bread with 1 Tbl vinaigrette. Arrange 1 or 2 leaves Romaine lettuce in center of bread. Top with 1/2 c avocado salad, garnish with 1/2 oz cheese.

Makes 24 servings.

This recipe is courtesy of the California Avocado Commission.

SANDWICHES

Roasted Red Pepper and Avocado Sandwich

2 Ciabatta loaves, sliced in half lengthwise
1/2 c hummus, roasted garlic flavor
1 small jar roasted red peppers
1/2 ripe avocado, peeled, pitted and thinly sliced
Juice of 1/2 fresh lemon
Salt and fresh black pepper to taste
1/2 Roma tomato, sliced thinly
2 small leaves lettuce

Evenly spread roasted garlic flavored hummus over 4 halves of sliced Ciabatta bread. Top with roasted red peppers and avocado slices. Drizzle fresh lemon juice over avocado slices then season to taste with salt and pepper.
Layer tomato slices and lettuce leaves over avocados and place Ciabatta slices together. Slice sandwich in half, fasten each half with a toothpick and serve immediately.

Makes 2 sandwiches.

Avocado Asparagus Sandwich

24 asparagus spears
1 large ripe avocado, peeled and pitted
1 Tbl fresh lime juice
1 clove garlic, minced
1 1/2 c cooked long-grain rice
3 Tbl plain non-fat yogurt
3 fresh whole-wheat tortillas, 10-in diameter
1/3 c fresh cilantro, chopped finely
2 Tbl red onion, chopped finely

In a medium saucepan, bring about 2-inches of water to boil. Place asparagus in a steamer basket, cover and steam until just tender, about 5 minutes. Remove asparagus and immediately rinse in cold water to stop the cooking process. Drain thoroughly. In a small bowl, coarsely mash avocado and mix well with lime juice and minced garlic.

Cook rice per package instructions.

In another small bowl thoroughly mix plain yogurt with rice.

Using a large skillet warm tortillas over medium heat until softened.

Lay tortillas flat on a clean surface and evenly layer avocados, asparagus, rice and yogurt mixture, cilantro and red onion.

Fold in both sides of tortilla and wrap tightly. If made in advance, store wrapped in plastic in refrigerator for up to 1 hour. Warm to room temperature prior to serving. To serve, cut each wrap in half crosswise.

Makes 6 servings.

Chicken and Avocado Wraps

2 large fresh whole-wheat tortillas, warmed to soften
2 Tbl light mayonnaise
1 cooked chicken breast, chopped
1 ripe avocado, peeled, pitted and sliced
1/2 c cooked couscous
1/2 c Chinese cabbage
1/4 c bean sprouts
1/4 red onion, sliced finely
1/4 c low-fat cheddar cheese, grated
Cracked black pepper to taste

Warm tortillas in large skillet over medium heat or in microwave. Lay tortillas flat on clean workspace. Spread mayonnaise thinly onto tortillas and top with chicken breast, avocado, couscous, cabbage, bean sprouts, red onion, cheese and cracked black pepper. Tuck both ends of tortillas inward and roll tightly. Slice diagonally and serve immediately.

Makes 2 wraps.

Shredded Chicken Avocado Wraps

1 small white onion, chopped
2 skinless, boneless chicken breasts
2 Tbl unsalted butter
1 (16oz) can whole tomatoes
21/2 c water
1/2 tsp cayenne
1 tsp ground cumin
Salt and freshly ground black pepper to taste
1 cucumber, peeled and sliced
1 large ripe avocado, peeled, pitted and thinly sliced
2 Tbl fresh lime juice
4 large sun-dried tomato tortillas, warmed to soften
1 c fresh cilantro, chopped

In a 2-quart heavy saucepan cook chicken breast in butter over moderate heat about 5 minutes, melting butter. Drain tomatoes and use one packed cup (reserve remaining tomatoes for later). Stir tomatoes into chicken mixture with water, cayenne and cumin. Simmer over medium/low heat, covered, for one hour, or until chicken is tender, shredding easily with a fork. Remove chicken from water and shred on a clean surface. Salt and pepper to taste and set aside.

Place cucumber and avocado slices in a small bowl and toss with lime juice.

Lay tortillas flat and layer with chicken, avocado slices, cucumber slices and sprinkle with fresh cilantro. Fold in both ends and roll tightly. Serve immediately, sliced diagonally.

Makes 4 servings.

SANDWICHES

Avocado and Tomato Wraps

3 ripe avocados, peeled, pitted and coarsely mashed
1/4 c red onion, chopped
1/4 tsp garlic salt
1 tomato, chopped
1/4 c fresh cilantro, chopped
1 fresh jalapeño, seeded and chopped finely
4 fresh corn tortillas, heated to soften

Combine avocado, onion and garlic salt. Spread evenly over corn tortillas. Sprinkle with chopped tomato, cilantro and jalapeño. Fold in both ends of tortilla and roll tightly. Secure each wrap with a toothpick.
Serve immediately.

Makes 2 servings.

Crab and Avocado Salad Pita

2/3 c light mayonnaise
2 Tbl diced roasted red pepper
4 Tbl fresh lemon juice
Pinch of cayenne pepper
2 c lump crab meat, picked through for shells and cartilage
1 medium avocado, peeled, pitted and chopped
2 Tbl white onion, grated
Salt and ground white pepper to taste
4 whole-wheat pita pocket breads
1 cup alfalfa sprouts

In a blender puree mayonnaise, red pepper, 1 Tbl lemon juice and cayenne pepper. Set aside.

In a medium bowl toss together crab meat, avocado, white onion, remaining lemon juice, salt and pepper.

Cut the top third off the pita breads. Divide the crab meat mixture evenly among pita breads, drizzle with mayonnaise sauce and tuck some alfalfa sprouts into each stuffed pita.

Wrap tightly with wax paper and can keep chilled in refrigerator for up to 1 hour.

Makes 4 servings.

SANDWICHES

Cashew Chicken Avocado Wraps

2 c cooked chicken breast, chopped
1/3 c light mayonnaise
1/2 c fresh basil, chopped
2 Tbl fresh lime juice
1 tsp chili-garlic paste
4 (10in) fresh whole-wheat tortillas, warmed to soften
2 ripe avocados, peeled, pitted and sliced
1/2 c cashews, chopped
4 lettuce leaves

In a medium bowl mix mayonnaise, basil, lime juice and chili-garlic paste. Mix in chopped chicken.

Lay tortillas flat and spread chicken mix down the center of each tortilla. Layer avocado, cashews and lettuce leaves over chicken mixture. Fold both ends of tortillas in and roll tightly.

Chill 30 minutes, or up to 2 hours.

Slice diagonally to serve.

Makes 4 servings.

Southwestern Tortilla Wrap

2 fresh whole-wheat tortillas, warmed to soften
1/4 c cooked black beans
1/2 c chunky salsa
1/4 c low-fat cheddar cheese
1 medium ripe avocado, peeled, pitted and sliced
1/4 red onion, thinly sliced
1/2 c alfalfa sprouts

Lay tortillas flat on a clean surface. Spread black beans, then salsa. Sprinkle cheddar cheese and top with avocado slices, red onion and alfalfa sprouts. Fold both ends of the tortilla in and roll tightly. Slice diagonally into three even pieces. Secure with toothpicks and serve immediately.

Makes 2 servings.

SANDWICHES

Grilled Vegetable and Avocado Wrap

2 fresh whole-wheat tortillas, warmed to soften
1 Tbl extra-virgin olive oil
1/4 c zucchini, peeled, halved and sliced lengthwise
1/4 c red onion, thinly sliced
1/4 c mushrooms, thinly sliced
2 lettuce leaves
1/4 c low-fat cheddar cheese, grated
1 medium ripe avocado, peeled, pitted and sliced
3 Tbl balsamic vinaigrette

In a medium skillet, heat olive oil over medium/high heat. Slice vegetables and sauté in heated olive oil, stirring frequently until lightly browned, about 8 to 10 minutes. Lay warmed tortillas on a flat, clean surface. Place a lettuce leaf on each tortilla and top with cheese, avocado and grilled vegetables. Sprinkle dressing over the top of each open wrap.
Fold both ends of tortillas in and roll tightly.
Slice diagonally and serve warm. Makes 2 servings.

Grow your own!

Here are some tips from the California Avocado Commission:

- Avocado trees like a soil ph of 6 to 6.5.
- These are shallow-rooted trees that like good aeration.
- They do best with a woody mulch about 2" in diameter. Use about 1/3 cubic yard per tree, but keep it about 6 to 8 inches away from the trunk.
- Take care not to disturb the delicate root system when planting. If the ball is root-bound, carefully loosen the soil around the edge and clip any roots that are going in circles.
- The ideal time to plant is March through June. During the summer there is a risk of sun damage and the young trees may not take up enough water.
- The hole should be as deep as the root ball and just a bit wider.
- Once gently planted, fill the hole with soil. Do not use gravel or potting mix.
- The major nutrients needed by avocado trees are Nitrogen, Phosphorus and Potassium (NPK) in a 7-4-2 fertilizer and Zinc.
- Feed young trees 1/2 to 1 pound of actual nitrogen per tree per year.
- When watering, soak the soil as well and then allow it to dry somewhat before watering again.
- Typically trees need to be watered two to three times a week. A mature tree will take about 20 gallons of water a day.

This information was provided by Dr. Mary Lu Arpaia, Extension Subtropical Horticulturist, Kearny Agriculture Center, Parlier, CA and Dr. Ben Faber, Farm Advisor, Soils and Water, Avocados and Subtropicals, Ventura County, CA.

SANDWICHES

Salads

Red Bean and Avocado Salad

1 c red kidney beans, cooked
4 leaves Romaine lettuce, sliced
1 large ripe avocado, peeled, pitted
and sliced
1 tomato, diced
3 Tbl red wine vinaigrette
Mustard powder, salt and freshly
ground black pepper to taste
4-6 whole-wheat tortillas

In a medium bowl, mix red kidney beans, lettuce, sliced avocado and diced tomatoes together. Drizzle with red wine vinaigrette, mustard powder, salt and pepper and toss to mix.
Roll tortillas into a cone shape and fasten with a toothpick. Fill with salad and serve.

Makes 2 servings.

SALAD

Avocado Salad

2 ripe avocados, peeled, pitted and balled
6 romaine lettuce leaves
1 tsp salt
1/2 tsp white pepper
1/2 tsp dried oregano
1 clove garlic, minced
1 sprig fresh thyme
2/3 c olive oil
1 Tbl red wine
1 Tbl vinegar
1 Tbl lemon juice

Peel and pit avocados and scoop out avocado fruit with rounded spoon, shaping fruit into balls. Place the avocado balls onto two plates lines with romaine lettuce leaves. In a small bowl whisk together salt, white pepper, dried oregano, thyme, olive oil, red wine, vinegar and lemon juice.
Pour over avocados and serve immediately.

Makes 2 servings.

Avocado Pineapple Salad

1 large ripe avocado, peeled, pitted and diced
1 can diced pineapple or 1 fresh pineapple, peeled, cored and diced
1/4 c fresh cilantro, chopped
1/4 white onion, thinly sliced
1 c shredded romaine lettuce
1/2 c shredded spinach
Juice of 1 lime

In a large bowl toss diced avocado, pineapple chunks, fresh cilantro, white onion, romaine lettuce and spinach.
Top with lime juice and serve chilled.

Makes 2 to 3 servings.

SALAD

Grilled Shrimp Avocado Salad

1 lb shrimp, peeled, deveined, tails on bamboo skewers, marinated for 1 hour

Marinade Ingredients
1 lime, juice and zest only
1/2 c fresh lime juice
2 cloves garlic, minced
1 tsp Thai chili, minced
1 Tbl rice wine vinegar
1 tsp sugar
1/4 c extra-virgin olive oil
1 tsp cayenne pepper

Salad Ingredients
6 ears grilled corn, kernels shaved from the cob
1/2 c Vidalia onion, diced
1 whole roasted red pepper, diced
1 tomato, seeded and diced
1/2 c fresh cilantro, chopped
2 cloves garlic, minced
1 jalapeño, seeded and diced small
2 large avocado, peeled, pitted and diced
Salt and freshly ground black pepper to taste

Dressing Ingredients
1 Tbl extra-virgin olive oil
2 Tbl red wine vinegar
1/2 tsp chopped parsley

Mix all marinade ingredients in a large Ziploc bag, add shrimp and let sit for 1 hour.
Briskly whisk all dressing ingredients in a small bowl
Toss salad ingredients in large bowl and drizzle with dressing. Toss again to evenly coat with dressing, cover with plastic wrap and chill.
Heat grill to 400 degrees F.
Skewer shrimp, leaving enough room on one end to handle for turning. Season well

with salt and pepper. Grill 1 to 2 minutes, or until no longer opaque. Arrange shrimp on top of salad. Serve warm or cold.

Makes 2 to 3 servings.

SALAD

Italian Walnut and Avocado Salad

1 ripe avocado, peeled, pitted and diced
2 tsp lemon juice
1 c red leaf lettuce, shredded
1/2 c spinach, stemmed
2 Tbl chopped walnuts
Drizzle olive oil
1 Tbl red wine vinegar
Salt and freshly ground black pepper to taste

Combine diced avocado and lemon juice in a salad bowl and mix well. Add shredded red leaf lettuce, spinach leaves and chopped walnuts.
Drizzle with olive oil and red wine vinegar. Salt and freshly ground black pepper to taste and toss salad.
Serve chilled.

Makes 2 to 3 servings.

Jicama and Avocado Salad

Jalapeño Dressing Ingredients
1/4 c light mayonnaise
1/4 c low-fat sour cream
1 1/2 Tbl fresh jalapeño, diced
2 Tbl fat-free milk
1/2 tsp fresh lemon juice
1/8 tsp onion powder

Salad Ingredients
4 large lettuce leaves
2 c shredded jicama
1 large ripe avocado, peeled, pitted and diced
1/2 lemon, juiced

In a medium bowl, mix dressing ingredients and chill for an hour.
Arrange leaves of lettuce on four plates. Place jicama on plates. Squeeze lemon juice over diced avocados and place avocados on top of jicama.
Drizzle salad dressing over salad and serve.

Makes 3 to 4 servings.

SALAD

Leafy Lettuces Avocado Salad

1/2 head red leaf lettuce, cored and coarsely torn
1/2 head green leaf lettuce, cored and coarsely torn
1 lemon, juiced
Salt and freshly ground black pepper to taste
4 Tbl extra-virgin olive oil
1 large ripe avocado, peeled, pitted and thinly sliced
1/2 pint cherry tomatoes, quartered
1 Poblano chili, cored, seeded and thinly sliced
3 green onions, thinly sliced
2 Tbl fresh cilantro, chopped

In a large salad bowl, combine the lettuces.
In another bowl, whisk the lemon juice, salt and black pepper. Whisk in the oil, 1 table-spoon at a time until the mixture emulsifies.
Add slices of avocado to the lemon dressing, then tomatoes, Poblano chili, green onions and cilantro.
Pour dressing over mixed greens and serve immediately.

Makes 4 to 6 servings.

Mango and Avocado Salad

1 1/2 c cabbage, shredded
1/2 c cucumbers, diced
1 ripe mango, peeled, pitted and diced
1 red bell pepper, cored and diced
1 ripe avocado, peeled, pitted and diced
6 green onions, thinly sliced
1/2 c watercress, stemmed
5 Tbl fresh lime juice
1 clove garlic, minced
1 tsp salt
1/2 tsp cayenne pepper

In a salad bowl, combine shredded cabbage, diced cucumbers, diced mango, diced bell pepper, diced avocado, sliced green onions and stemmed watercress. Drizzle lime juice over salad top and toss in minced garlic, salt and cayenne pepper.
Serve chilled.

Makes 2 to 3 servings.

SALAD

Avocado Hot Pepper Sauce Salad

4 medium tomatoes
3 ripe avocados, peeled, pitted and mashed
1 Tbl onion, minced
1 tsp chili powder
2 to 4 drops hot pepper sauce
1 tsp salt
1 1/2 tsp fresh cilantro, chopped
8 leaves lettuce

Peel tomatoes and cut off tops. Scoop out pulp in the center leaving hollow space, reserving pulp.
Dice tomato pulp into small squares. Mash avocados and in small bowl mix well with onion, chili powder, hot pepper sauce, salt, cilantro and reserved tomato.
Stuff tomatoes with avocado mixture and serve on beds of crisp lettuce.

Makes 4 servings.

Endive, Pea and Avocado Salad

Dressing Ingredients
1/2 c extra-virgin olive oil
2 Tbl white wine vinegar
Pinch of salt
Pinch of sugar
Pinch of white pepper
1/2 c chopped parsley

Salad Ingredients
1 (9oz) package frozen baby peas (or small can, rinsed and drained)
2 heads endive lettuce, shredded
1 c fresh spinach, stemmed
3 ripe avocados, peeled, pitted and diced
1 fresh lemon, juiced

In a medium-mixing bowl combine olive oil, white wine vinegar, salt, sugar, white pepper and parsley. Mix well with a wire whisk. Set dressing aside.
Place frozen peas in a colander and pour boiling water over them to thaw. Drain well. In a salad bowl, mix peas, lettuce, spinach and avocados. Squeeze lemon over avocados. Toss with dressing and serve. Makes 2 to 3 servings.

SALAD

Shrimp and Avocado Salad

1/4 c grapeseed oil
1/4 c white wine vinegar
3 garlic cloves, minced
1/2 lb medium shrimp, cooked, peeled and deveined
4-8 leaves red leaf lettuce
2 ripe avocados
2 Tbl chopped roasted walnuts
1 Tbl fresh cilantro, chopped
Lemon slices for garnish

Combine oil, vinegar and garlic in a medium bowl. Whisk to mix. Chop shrimp into 1/2 inch pieces and add to oil mixture. Arrange leaves of lettuce onto 4 plates. Cut avocados in half, remove seeds and scoop a small amount of the inner fruit out to mix with shrimp. Using a large spoon, scoop avocado fruit out of shell, careful to keep intact. Place avocado halves on lettuce leaves. Spoon shrimp mixture into avocado shells and then sprinkle with roasted walnuts and cilantro. Serve with lemon slices for garnish.

Makes 4 servings.

Crab Meat and Avocado Salad

Sauce Ingredients
1 Tbl extra-virgin olive oil
1 ripe mango, peeled, pitted and diced
Salt and freshly ground black pepper to taste
1/4 c water
1 tsp fresh lemon juice
Dash of chili powder

Salad Ingredients
1 lb fresh lump crab meat, picked through for shell pieces or cartilage
1 Tbl fresh cilantro, finely chopped
2 tsp mint leaves, finely chopped
1 Tbl green onions, thinly sliced
1 1/2 Tbl fresh lime juice
3 Tbl extra-virgin olive oil
Hot pepper sauce to taste
Salt and freshly ground black pepper to taste
1 medium mango, peeled, pitted and diced
1 firm, but ripe avocado, peeled, pitted and diced
1 Tbl red onion, finely chopped

1 large ruby-red grapefruit, peeled and sectioned for garnish

Heat olive oil in a small skillet over medium heat. Add mango and season with salt, pepper and chili powder. Cook, stirring constantly for about 3 minutes, or until fruit is very tender. Add water, bring to a boil and then remove from heat. Stir in lemon juice. Pour mixture into a blender and puree until smooth. Pour mixture into bowl and chill.

Salad Ingredients
In a large bowl, mix crab meat, 2 tsp cilantro, 1 tsp mint, green onions, 1 Tbl fresh lime juice, 2 Tbl olive oil, hot pepper sauce, salt and pepper. Toss gently.
In a medium bowl, mix mango, avocado, red onion, 1 Tbl olive oil, 1/2 Tbl lime juice, remaining cilantro and mint leaves, hot pepper sauce, salt and black pepper to taste.

SALAD

Mix gently.

Using small dessert bowls for individual molds, layer the crab mixture and the mango-avocado mixture. Chill in the refrigerator for 1 to 2 hours.

When you are ready to serve, gently remove salads from molds onto individual plates. Serve sauce on the side. Garnish with cilantro leaves and arrange grapefruit sections around salads.

Makes 3 to 4 servings.

Walnut and Avocado Salad

2 ripe avocados, peeled, pitted and sliced lengthwise
4 Tbl fresh lemon juice
1 Tbl chopped olives
1 Tbl crushed walnuts
5 coriander seeds, crushed
1 tsp mustard
Salt and pepper to taste
3 Tbl extra-virgin olive oil

Sprinkle avocados with some lemon juice. Mix 2 Tbl lemon juice, olives, walnuts, coriander seeds and mustard in a small bowl. Season to taste with salt and freshly ground black pepper and beat into the olive oil.
Fan avocados out on a plate and drizzle with the sauce.

Makes 2 servings.

SALAD

Rice and Avocado Salad

3 c long-grain rice or brown rice, cooked
2 c cooked chicken breasts, chopped
2 ripe avocados, peeled, pitted and diced
1 c diagonally sliced celery
1/2 green bell pepper, cut into julienned strips
1/2 c white onion, minced
3 Tbl fresh lemon juice
2 Tbl extra-virgin olive oil
1 1/2 tsp sugar
1/4 tsp white pepper
1 clove garlic, minced
Hot pepper sauce to taste
1 tsp extra-virgin olive oil
Salad greens
Tomato wedges to garnish

Combine rice, cooked chicken, avocados, celery, green bell pepper and onion in a large bowl.

Place olive oil, sugar, white pepper, garlic, hot pepper sauce and olive oil in a medium mixing bowl and whisk well. Pour dressing over rice mixture and toss well. Cover and refrigerate for 1 to 2 hours before serving. Serve on salad greens and garnish with tomato slices.

Makes 4 to 6 servings.

Grapefruit Avocado Salad

2 whole grapefruits, peeled and sectioned
2 large ripe avocados, peeled, pitted and diced
1/2 lime, juiced
1/2 c cashews, chopped
1/2 c coleslaw salad dressing

Place grapefruit sections in a medium mixing bowl. Add avocados, lime juice, cashews and drizzle with dressing. Toss gently and serve.

Makes 3 to 4 servings.

SALAD

Citrus Avocado Salad

Salad Ingredients
8 c torn salad greens
2 grapefruits, peeled and sectioned
2 medium naval oranges, peeled and sectioned
2 medium ripe avocados, peeled, pitted and diced
1 small red onion, thinly sliced and separated into rings

Dressing
1/2 c extra-virgin olive oil
2 Tbl sugar
2 Tbl fresh lemon juice
11/2 tsp poppy seeds
1/2 tsp salt
1/4 tsp ground mustard
1/4 tsp grated onion

In a large salad bowl, gently toss salad greens, grapefruits sections, orange sections, avocados and red onion.

In a small bowl, briskly whisk olive oil, sugar, lemon juice, poppy seeds, salt, ground mustard and grated onion.

Drizzle dressing over salad and toss to coat.

Makes 8 to 10 servings.

Broccoli and Avocado Salad

1 small bunch broccoli, salted to taste
1 large ripe avocado, peeled, pitted and thinly sliced
1/2 lemon, juiced
1 tsp spicy mustard
1/2 tsp garlic, chopped finely
1 Tbl red wine vinegar
Freshly ground black pepper to taste
3 Tbl extra-virgin olive oil

Chop broccoli into bite-size pieces, then rinse and drain. Place broccoli in a medium saucepan and add just enough water to cover. Cover and bring water to a boil. Cook 2 to 5 minutes until just tender but still crisp. Remove and rinse broccoli under cool water, draining well. Place broccoli in a small bowl and refrigerate.
Cut avocado into thin strips and squeeze lemon juice over slices. Set aside.
Combine mustard, garlic, red wine vinegar, black pepper and olive oil in a small bowl and whisk until thoroughly mixed.
Arrange cooled broccoli and treated avocado strips onto serving plates and drizzle dressing over the top. Serve immediately.

Makes 1 to 2 servings.

SALAD

Watercress Avocado Salad

Dressing Ingredients
2 Tbl shallots, finely chopped
3 Tbl fresh lime juice
2 Tbl fresh orange juice
4 Tbl sherry vinegar
1 tsp honey
1/4 c extra-virgin olive oil
1 tsp freshly grated nutmeg
Salt and freshly ground black pepper to taste

Salad Ingredients
1 bunch watercress, cleaned
2 chayotes, cooked and diced into 1-inch cubes
1 cup ripe papaya, peeled, pitted and cubed
2 medium ripe avocados, peeled, pitted and cubed
Salt and freshly ground black pepper to taste
1/2 c fried plantain slivers for garnish

In a medium bowl, combine all dressing ingredients and vigorously whisk until well mixed. Cover and refrigerate.
In a large salad bowl, combine watercress with a small amount of dressing. Mix gently. Place watercress on a serving dish, shaking off any excess dressing. Next repeat the process with the chayote and a small amount of dressing. Add coated chayote to the watercress, also removing any excess dressing. Repeat process with papayas and avocados. When watercress, chayote, papaya and avocados have been coated with dressing and placed on serving plates, salt and black pepper to taste. Garnish with fried plantain slivers and serve immediately.

Makes 2 to 3 servings.

Shrimp, Papaya and Avocado Salad

1 1/4 lbs large shrimp
1 medium papaya, peeled, pitted and sliced
2 large avocados, peeled, pitted and thinly sliced
3 Tbl extra-virgin olive oil
3 Tbl fresh cilantro, chopped
2 Tbl fresh lime juice
Salt and freshly ground black pepper to taste
1/4 c whole fresh cilantro leaves to garnish

Place 2 cups of water in a large skillet and bring to a boil. Add shrimp and simmer for about 30 seconds. Remove from heat and allow shrimp to sit in hot water for about 30 minutes. Peel shrimp and discard the shells. Reserve shrimp in a bowl.

Place papaya and avocado slices on a serving platter, alternating and overlapping.

In a small bowl, briskly whisk olive oil, cilantro, lime juice, salt and pepper until well mixed. Combine half the dressing with the shrimp, mixing well and reserve the remaining.

Place shrimp over avocado and papaya slices and drizzle remaining dressing over the top.

Serve immediately.

Makes 6 servings.

SALAD

Black Bean and Avocado Salad

1 (16oz) can black beans, rinsed and drained well
2 vine ripened tomatoes, diced
1 red onion, diced
1 Tbl pickled jalapeños, diced
1 large ripe avocado, peeled, pitted and diced
1 ripe lime, juiced
1 Tbl olive oil
Salt and freshly ground black pepper to taste

Using a colander, rinse and drain black beans. Dice tomatoes, onion, jalapeño and avocado. In a large salad bowl, mix black beans, tomatoes, onion, jalapeños, avocado, lime juice and olive oil. Toss until all ingredients are coated. Salt and pepper to taste.

Makes 3 to 4 servings.

Chickpea Avocado Salad

1 large ripe avocado, peeled, pitted and diced
1 (16oz) can chickpeas, rinsed and drained well
1/4 c banana peppers
1/2 red bell pepper, thinly sliced
1/2 red onion, thinly sliced
2 Tbl cider vinegar
Salt and freshly ground black pepper to taste

Drain and rinse the chickpeas in cold water.
In a medium mixing bowl, combine avocado, chickpeas, banana peppers, red bell pepper onion and cider vinegar. Salt and black pepper to taste and toss to mix flavors.

Makes 3 to 4 servings.

SALAD

Tangerine Avocado Salad

Dressing Ingredients
1/3 c extra-virgin olive oil
1 tsp grated tangerine peel
1/4 c freshly squeezed tangerine juice
1 Tbl sugar
2 Tbl lemon juice
1/2 tsp ground mustard
1/4 tsp salt

Salad Ingredients
3 tangerines, peeled and sliced
2 ripe avocados, peeled, pitted and sliced
6 thin slices red onion, separated into rings
Salad greens

Place all dressing ingredients in a glass jar, seal and shake vigorously.
Using 6 salad plates, arrange tangerines, avocados and onion rings on top of salad greens. Drizzle dressing over the top and serve immediately.

Makes 6 servings.

Carrot Avocado Salad

1 lb medium carrots
1/2 c fresh cilantro, chopped
1/4 c red onion, chopped finely
3 Tbl extra-virgin olive oil
2 Tbl fresh lemon juice
1 small garlic clove, chopped finely
3/4 tsp salt
1/4 tsp freshly ground black pepper
1 large firm-ripe avocado, peeled, pitted and diced

Halve carrots lengthwise and cut diagonally into 2-inch pieces. Cook carrots in a saucepan of boiling salt-water until just tender, 5 to 6 minutes. Drain in a colander and transfer to a bowl of ice and cold water to stop cooking process. Let stand 5 minutes, drain again and pat dry.

While carrots cool, briskly whisk together cilantro, onion, olive oil, lemon juice, garlic, salt and pepper until well mixed.

Combine carrots and avocados in salad bowl, drizzle dressing over top and toss to mix. Serve immediately.

Makes 4 servings.

SALAD

Apple and Avocado Salad
with Tangerine Dressing

Dressing Ingredients
4 mandarin oranges, juiced
1/2 lemon, juiced
1/2 tsp lemon zest
1 clove garlic, minced
2 Tbl extra-virgin olive oil
Salt to taste

Salad Ingredients
1 c baby greens
1/4 c red onion, chopped
1/2 c walnuts, chopped
1/3 c crumbled blue cheese
2 tsp lemon zest
1 apple, peeled, cored and sliced
1 ripe-firm avocado, peeled, pitted and diced

In a large bowl, toss baby greens, red onion, walnuts, blue cheese and lemon zest. Add apple and avocado just before serving.

In a glass jar mix mandarin orange juice, lemon juice, lemon zest, garlic, olive oil and salt. Cover and vigorously shake until well mixed.

Drizzle over salad and serve immediately.

Makes 2 to 3 servings.

Apple, Avocado and Hearts of Palm Salad

Dressing Ingredients
3/4 c low-fat mayonnaise
1/4 c ketchup
2 tsp white sugar
1 lemon, juiced
1/4 tsp paprika
1 pinch ground black pepper
2 Tbl freshly chopped chives

Salad Ingredients
3 cups mixed salad greens
1 large ripe-firm avocado, peeled, pitted and diced
2 Granny Smith apples, peeled, cored and thinly sliced
1/2 c coarsely chopped walnuts
1 cup sliced hearts of palm

In a medium bowl, briskly whisk mayonnaise, ketchup, sugar, lemon juice, paprika and black pepper. Stir in chives and set aside.

In a large salad bowl, toss salad greens, walnuts and hearts of palm. Add avocado and apple slices just before serving.

Drizzle with dressing and toss to coat.
Serve immediately.

Makes 6 to 8 servings.

SALAD

Apple, Beet and Avocado Salad

Dressing Ingredients
3/4 c apple cider
2/3 c cider vinegar
1/2 c extra-virgin olive oil
1/2 tsp salt
1/2 tsp freshly ground black pepper
1 tsp prepared mustard
1/4 tsp celery seed

Salad Ingredients
3 medium fresh beets
1 c mixed salad greens
1 red onion, sliced into thin rings
1 apple, peeled, cored and thinly sliced
1/2 ripe-firm avocado, peeled, pitted and sliced
1/2 c toasted walnuts, chopped

Preheat oven to 400 degrees F. Wash beets and lay on a baking dish with 1/4 cup of water. Cover and bake for 1 hour or until tender. Remove from oven and set aside to cool.

Whisk together the apple cider, vinegar, olive oil, salt, pepper, mustard and celery seed in a small bowl.

Peel and slice beets, mix with vinaigrette and refrigerate for 30 minutes.

Divide greens among four salad plates. Drain beets and reserve dressing. Arrange overlapping layers of beets over salad greens, add onions, apples and avocados. Drizzle salads with dressing, sprinkle with walnuts and serve immediately.

Makes 2 to 3 servings.

Avocado, Crab and Grapefruit Salad

4 ripe-firm avocado, peeled and pitted
1 lb crab meat, picked through for shell pieces and cartilage, and diced
1/2 c pecans, chopped
3/4 c light mayonnaise
2 tsp ketchup
Dash of Worcestershire sauce
8 lettuce leaves
2 large grapefruits, peeled and sectioned
2 hard-boiled eggs, chopped
1/2 c black olives, sliced

Cook crab meat and combine in a medium bowl with pecans, mayonnaise, ketchup and Worcestershire sauce. Mix well.

Slice avocados in half and remove the seeds and skins. Scoop crab mixture into avocado pits. Arrange lettuce leaves on 4 serving plates and place filled avocado slices onto lettuce. Place grapefruit sections around filled avocados and garnish with eggs and black olives.

Makes 4 servings.

SALAD

Orange Avocado Salad
with Wasabi-Glazed Chicken Strips

4 skinless, boneless chicken breast halves
1 Tbl extra-virgin olive oil
Glaze Ingredients
1/2 c white sugar
1/4 c water
1/2 c red wine
1 c orange juice
1 tsp wasabi paste

Dressing Ingredients
1/4 c cider vinegar
3 Tbl extra-virgin olive oil

Salad Ingredients
1/2 tomato, diced
1/4 c red onion, thinly sliced and separated into rings
2 Tbl fresh cilantro, chopped
2 limes, juiced
2 ripe-firm avocados, peeled, pitted and diced
1 c mixed salad greens
Salt and pepper to taste
Hot pepper sauce to taste

Preheat oven to 400 degrees F.
Slice chicken into strips and cook in a skillet with olive oil over medium/high heat until done, about 8 to 10 minutes, stirring constantly.

In a large saucepan, heat sugar and water together over medium/high heat, stirring occasionally until caramelized to a deep amber color. Remove from heat and slowly add red wine. Return to heat and stir until all particles are dissolved. Stirring constantly add orange juice and wasabi paste, adjusting the amount to taste. Remove from heat. Brush chicken strips with glaze and then place on a baking sheet. Bake in preheated oven until thoroughly heated, about 5 to 7 minutes.

While chicken is warming, toss together tomato, red onion, cilantro, lime juice, avocados, salad greens and salt, pepper and hot pepper sauce to taste.

In a small bowl, combine cider vinegar and olive oil. Whisk until well mixed. Drizzle over salad and top with glazed chicken strips.

Serve immediately.

Makes 3 to 4 servings.

SALAD

Avocado, Watermelon and Spinach Salad

2 large ripe-firm avocados, peeled, pitted and diced
1 c watermelon, cubed
4 c fresh spinach leaves, stemmed
1 c balsamic vinaigrette dressing

In a salad bowl, toss together avocados, watermelon and spinach leaves.
Drizzle with dressing, salt and pepper to taste and toss to mix flavors.
Serve immediately.

Makes 4 to 6 servings.

Alaskan Salmon and Avocado Pasta Salad

Salad Ingredients
6 oz penne pasta, cooked
2 Tbl French dressing
1 (14 3/4 oz) can Alaskan salmon
1 bundle green onions, sliced thinly
1 large red bell pepper, thinly sliced
3 Tbl fresh cilantro, chopped finely

Dressing Ingredients
1 lime, juiced
1 Tbl tomato paste
1/2 c low-fat sour cream
2 Tbl light mayonnaise
Paprika to taste
3 ripe-firm avocados, peeled, pitted and diced
Lettuce leaves to serve on

SALAD

Cook pasta, drain and toss in large bowl with French dressing. Allow to cool.
Drain and flake the salmon. Add to pasta along with green onions, sliced bell pepper
and cilantro.
In a small bowl whisk together lime juice, tomato paste, sour cream, mayonnaise and
paprika.
Toss salad together with dressing until well mixed. Salt and pepper to taste. Serve
salad on bed of lettuce leaves garnished with paprika.

Makes 4 to 6 servings.

Almond and Avocado Rice Salad

Dressing Ingredients
4 Tbl extra-virgin olive oil
2 Tbl fresh lemon juice
1/2 tsp salt
1 tsp sugar

Salad Ingredients
1 c brown rice, cooked
Pinch of salt
1 tsp salad oil
4 green onions, chopped
1 Tbl parsley, chopped
6 cherry tomatoes, halved
1/4 c toasted almonds, slivered
1 large ripe-firm avocado, peeled, pitted and sliced

In a small bowl, briskly whisk all dressing ingredients together until well mixed.
Cook rice as directed, adding a pinch of salt and 1 tsp salad oil to the water. When rice is cooked, rinse with cold water until it has cooled. Drain well. Place rice in a large salad bowl and combine with green onions, 1/2 Tbl chopped parsley and half the prepared dressing. Stir until well mixed.
Place a layer of the rice mixture on the serving dish and arrange halved tomatoes around edges. Sprinkle with toasted almond slivers.
Cut avocado into fan-shaped slivers and arrange on top of rice. Pour remaining dressing onto avocado slivers and top with remaining parsley. Can refrigerate, covered for up to 6 hours before serving.

Makes 1 serving.

History, Health and Home

The avocado has a history as rich as its velvety, nutty flavor and is an indisputable leader in nutrient rich composition. The avocado should be a staple ingredient in every home.

Avocados have been revered throughout history for their healing powers. Today, we know that they are jam-packed with nutrients, a great source of antioxidants, even known to lower cholesterol. All parts of the avocado tree have been used medicinally. The leaves and bark have traditionally been used as an astringent and to provide cough relief. The fruit pulp is a natural emollient, as well as being nutrient-packed. The seed has even been used as an antibiotic.

Today, due to an increasing recognition of the harmful effects of additives and preservatives, the avocado is gaining popularity in the cosmetic industry, as well as the food industry. Avocado cosmetics are biodegradable and many consumers are now favoring more basic and natural ingredients. Avocados are known for their softening, smoothing abilities and their notable absorption.

The Centers for Disease Control and Prevention reports between 10-15 percent of children between ages 6-17 are considered overweight. Less than 20 percent eat the recommended number of servings of fruits and vegetables. The USDA reports that only 2 percent of children meet recommendations of the Food Guide Pyramid.

Americans spend nearly 40 billion each year on diet products. FTC studies have found that 55 percent of weight-loss ads contain false or unsupported claims. Contrary to past assumptions, the avocado can be a great contribution to a weight-loss program or just a well-balanced diet for several reasons.

• Its mono unsaturated fat speeds up the basal metabolic rate as compared with saturated fat.

• The high fat content found in the avocado gives a faster feeling of fullness, reducing overeating.

• The richness of its vitamin and mineral content makes the diet more wholesome and satisfying.

The Main Dish

Guacamole Enchiladas and Sauce

2 large ripe avocados, peeled, pitted and coarsely mashed
Salt and black pepper to taste
1/8 c red onion, chopped finely
Dash of garlic powder
6 fresh corn tortillas, warmed to soften
1/2 c low-fat cheddar cheese, grated
1/2 c low-fat Monterey Jack cheese, grated

Sauce Ingredients
1 c chicken broth (can substitute vegetable broth for vegetarian)
1/2 can diced tomatoes, drained
1 sm can tomato sauce
2 tsp red onion, diced finely
1 sm can green chilies, chopped
Dash of salt and pepper
Cornstarch as thickening agent

Preheat oven to 400 degrees F.

Coarsely mash avocados and salt and pepper to taste. In a small bowl, mix avocado with onion and garlic powder.

Warm tortillas using skillet or microwave to soften.

Lay tortillas flat and divide avocado mixture evenly between tortillas. Fold both ends of tortillas in and roll tightly.

Place filled tortillas in small glass baking dish and sprinkle with half the cheeses.

In a small saucepan, mix broth, diced tomatoes, tomato sauce, red onion and green chilies. Salt and freshly ground black pepper to taste. Cook over medium/high heat, stirring frequently until thickened, about 8 to 10 minutes. Add cornstarch to reach desired thickness.

Pour sauce over avocado enchiladas, then top with remaining cheeses.

Bake in preheated oven for 10 to 12 minutes, or until cheese is melted.

Makes 2 to 3 servings.

MAINS

Chicken Avocado Pizza

2 ripe avocado, peeled, pitted and diced
1 Tbl fresh cilantro, chopped
1 Tbl fresh lime juice
Salt to taste
4 small prepared pizza crusts or 4 flatbread/tortilla pizza crusts
1/4 c olive oil
1 clove garlic, peeled
2 boneless, skinless chicken breasts, cooked, diced and lightly salted
1 c cherry tomatoes, quartered
1 c low-fat Monterey Jack cheese, grated
Pinch of cayenne pepper

Preheat broiler.
In a food processor or blender combine avocado, cilantro, lime juice and salt. Puree until smooth. Cover and set aside.
Brush pizza crust with olive oil. Cut garlic clove in half and rub pizza crust with cut side for flavor.
Spread avocado mixture evenly over crust, then arrange chicken and tomatoes on top. Sprinkle with cheese and season lightly with cayenne pepper. Place pizza on baking sheet or preheated pizza stone and broil for 2 to 5 minutes, until cheese melts and crust is lightly browned.

Makes 4 personal pizzas.

Salmon with Avocado and Cilantro Salsa

2 lbs salmon fillets
Extra-virgin olive oil
1 large ripe-firm avocado, peeled, pitted and diced
1 ripe tomato, diced
1 Tbl fresh cilantro, chopped
1 lemon, juiced
1/2 c cider vinegar
1/4 c olive oil
Salt and freshly ground black pepper to taste.

Salmon should be filleted, then cut into 8oz portions. Place salmon pieces between plastic wrap and then lightly pound pieces until about 1/8 inch thick.
Heat a large skillet coated with olive oil until it begins to smoke. Quickly place a piece of salmon inside, sautéing 30 seconds on each side. Repeat until all salmon is lightly sautéed.
In a small bowl, combine avocado, tomato, cilantro, lemon juice, cider vinegar and olive oil. Salt and freshly ground black pepper to taste. Mix well.
Spoon salsa onto sautéed salmon to serve.

Makes 4 servings.

MAINS

Tofu Scrambled Burrito with Avocado Salsa

1 tsp garlic, minced
1 tsp extra-virgin olive oil
5 green onions, chopped
2 large carrots, grated
2 zucchini, grated
1 lb firm Tofu, crumbled
1/2 c roasted sunflower seeds
2 large whole-wheat tortillas, warmed to soften

Salsa Ingredients
1 ripe avocado, peeled, pitted and coarsely mashed
1/2 tomato, diced
1 tsp fresh lemon juice
1 tsp fresh cilantro, chopped finely
Salt and freshly ground black pepper to taste

In a medium skillet, sauté garlic in heated olive oil for 3 to 4 minutes until golden brown. Add green onions, carrots and zucchini and cook another 3 to 4 minutes, stirring constantly. Add tofu and sunflower seeds, stirring and cooking another 3 minutes; remove from heat.

In a small bowl, coarsely mash avocado and combine with tomato, lemon juice and chopped cilantro.

Warm tortilla on skillet or in microwave. Fill warmed tortilla with sautéed Tofu mixture and top with avocado salsa. Wrap tightly and serve immediately.

Makes 2 burritos.

Avocado, Papaya Salsa Chicken

Marinade Ingredients
1/2 c olive oil
1 c red wine vinegar
1 tsp garlic salt
1 tsp parsley
1 tsp salt
1 tsp freshly ground black pepper
2 tsp fresh orange juice

Salsa Ingredients
2 medium ripe avocados, peeled, pitted and chopped
1 small ripe papaya, peeled, seeded and chopped
1/3 c fresh lime juice
2 medium tomatoes, diced
2 green onions, thinly sliced
2 Tbl sugar
2 Tbl extra-virgin olive oil
1 Tbl snipped parsley
1 Tbl snipped fresh basil
Hot pepper sauce to taste

4 skinless, boneless chicken breast

MAINS

In a glass baking dish, briskly whisk all marinade ingredients. Coat both sides of chicken breasts and let site for 30 minutes to 1 hour. Grill chicken, brushing with marinade over medium heat until done, about 12 to 15 minutes.
In a 1-quart container with a lid, toss avocados and papaya with lime juice. Add tomatoes, green onions, sugar, olive oil, parsley, basil and hot pepper sauce.
Smother grilled chicken breast with avocado and papaya salsa and serve.

Makes 4 servings.

Orange Avocado Chicken

6 boneless, skinless chicken breast halves
1/4 c butter or margarine, melted
1 tsp grated orange rind
1 c fresh orange juice
1/2 c red onion, chopped
3/4 tsp salt
1 tsp paprika
1/2 tsp ground ginger
1/2 tsp dried whole tarragon, crushed
1 tsp cornstarch
2 oranges, peeled and sliced crosswise
1 large ripe avocado, peeled, pitted and sliced

Brown chicken in butter in large skillet over medium heat. Add orange rind, 1/2 c orange juice, red onion, salt, paprika, ginger and tarragon. Reduce heat to low and simmer, covered for about 50 minutes, or until chicken is tender. Remove chicken to serving dish and cover to keep warm.

Add remaining 1/2 c orange juice and cornstarch to skillet with pan drippings. Cook over low heat, stirring constantly, until thickened.

On serving dishes, arrange chicken with avocado slices, pouring orange sauce over chicken before serving.

Makes 6 servings.

Vegetables with Avocado Aioli

Vegetable Ingredients
1 lemon, halved
12 baby artichokes
1 lb young carrots, tops trimmed to 1 inch
1/2 lb thin green beans
1/2 lb sugar snap peas
12 small red skinned new potatoes
12 small beets

Avocado Aioli
2 ripe avocados, peeled, pitted and mashed
2 Tbl fresh lime juice
1 large clove garlic, minced
2 Tbl extra-virgin olive oil
1/4 c fresh cilantro, chopped
Salt and freshly ground black pepper
6 hard-boiled eggs, sliced lengthwise
2 Tbl fresh parsley, chopped coarsely

To cook the vegetables squeeze the lemon halves into a medium bowl and fill with water. Trim the artichoke stems and cut about 1/2 inch off the tops. Remove any tough outer leaves at the base and snip the points from the remaining leaves with scissors. Toss the artichokes into the acidulated water.

Bring a large pot of water to a boil. Add the artichokes and boil until tender when pierced, 15 to 20 minutes. Remove with a slotted spoon and drain well. In the same pot, boil the remaining vegetables, one at a time, until just tender; remove each batch with a slotted spoon as it's done.

To make the Avocado Aioli, halve the avocados. Scoop the flesh into a bowl. Mash with the lime juice and garlic. Scrape into a food processor and puree. While blending, drizzle in the oil. Scrape the puree into a bow. Fold in the cilantro and season with salt and pepper. Refrigerate for up to 2 hours.

To serve, arrange the vegetables and eggs on a large platter. Sprinkle the parsley over all. Spoon aioli into a bowl and serve along side.

Makes 6 to 8 servings.

MAINS

Bean and Avocado Burritos

7 fresh spinach tortillas
1 1/4 c chopped onion
2 cloves garlic, minced
1 Tbl olive oil
1/2 tsp salt
1 c shredded low-fat Monterey
Jack cheese

Soak beans overnight. Empty water and place beans in 4 cups fresh water in large saucepan. Bring to a boil, then reduce heat and simmer, covered for about 1 1/2 hours or until beans are very tender. Drain beans, but keep cooking liquid.

For filling, in large skillet, sauté onion and garlic in hot olive oil until tender. Remove from heat. Stir in drained beans and salt. Mash bean mixture, adding reserved cooking liquid (about 1/3 c) to get desired consistency.

Spoon filling into warmed tortilla, top with cheese and chopped tomato. Roll tortillas and arrange burritos on baking sheet. Cover and heat in oven at 350 degrees F for 10 minutes. Uncover and bake another 5 minutes more.

Serve burritos with chopped avocado, additional chopped tomato and salsa.

Makes 6 servings.

Avocado and Squash Burritos

2-dozen whole-wheat tortillas
1 red onion, sliced
1 lb broccoli, chopped
1/4 lb mushrooms, sliced
4-5 zucchini squash, sliced
2 large tomatoes, chopped
Guacamole
Salsa

Place onion, broccoli, mushrooms, squash and tomatoes in large skillet and add a few tablespoons of salsa. Mix and cover, simmering over medium heat for about 20 minutes. Stir frequently. Scoop vegetables into warm tortillas and wrap. Serve with salsa and guacamole. Makes 8 to 10 servings.

MAINS

Grilled Chicken and Avocado Fajitas

4 fresh flour tortillas

Ingredients for chicken:
2 tsp olive oil
4 small skinless, boneless
chicken breasts
Salt to taste
Lemon pepper to taste

Preheat grill to medium-high. Brush chicken breasts with olive oil and season with salt and lemon pepper. Cook on the grill about 4 to 5 minutes each side, depending on the thickness of the breast. Transfer the cooked chicken to a cutting board and cut into small pieces.

In a small mixing bowl, combine the cream cheese, green onions, chili peppers and cilantro. Salt and pepper to taste.

Warm tortillas using method of choice and lay flat. Divide the cream cheese mixture among the tortillas, spreading it out in the center of each tortilla. Add chicken and top each with one slice of avocado and tomato. Roll tortilla. Makes 4 servings.

California Avocado Commission

"The California Avocado Commission was created to cost-effectively build value for the California avocado brand through demand-building programs including advertising, merchandising, foodservice, public relations and nutrition." They have been very successful in their endeavor and the value and demand of their healthy, tasty product continues to grow at an increasingly fast rate.

The newly-updated Food Pyramid from the United States Department of Agriculture (USDA), now titled MyPyramid proves yet again the importance of fruits and vegetables by visually communicating that they should be consumed more regularly than any other food group. Avocados are featured on the MyPyramid website and are listed as a healthy fruit choice.

The California Avocado Commission website, www.avocado.org contends that the avocado, on top of providing excellent health and nutrient benefits, also can be used to prevent weight gain and/or maintain a healthy weight. Here are just a few reasons:

- Like other fruits and vegetables, avocados provide satiety because of their water and fiber content. This increases the feeling of fullness and can be used as part of an effective weight loss/weight management plan.
- Naturally cholesterol-free avocados are a delicious and nutritious alternative to saturated fat-laden spreads, toppings and dips.

Choosing a California Avocado increases the intake of vitamins, minerals, fiber and other key nutrients, especially those that are often low in typical diets.

Avocados have also been found to lower chronic disease risks by lowering intake of saturated fats, trans fats, cholesterol and sodium. The California Avocado Commission contends that:

- Avocados offer mono unsaturated fat, which supports heart health.
- Avocados are sodium- and cholesterol-free and like other fruits and vegetables, avocados offer several vitamins, minerals and phytonutrients that contribute to overall health and wellness.
- Consuming generous amounts of fruits and vegetables has been linked to a reduction in risk for several diseases, including stroke and heart disease, type2 diabetes and some types of cancer.

Appetizers

Avocado Bread

2 c all-purpose flour
3/4 c sugar
1 1/2 tsp baking powder
1/2 tsp baking soda
1/2 tsp salt
1 large egg
1 medium avocado, mashed
1/2 c buttermilk
1/2 c pecans, chopped

Preheat oven to 375 degrees F. Generously grease a 9x5-in loaf pan. Combine flour, sugar, baking powder, baking soda and salt in a large mixing bowl. Mix thoroughly. In a separate bowl, beat together the egg and avocado. Stir in the buttermilk. Add to the dry ingredients and blend well. Stir in the pecans. Pour into the prepared pan and bake for 50 minutes to 1 hour, or until a wooden pick inserted into the center of the loaf comes out clean. Makes 1 loaf.

APPETIZERS

Bruschetta With California Avocados and Basil

1 California avocado, peeled, pitted and diced
1/2 lb Roma tomatoes, sliced lengthwise and diced
1/4 c red onion, diced
2 Tbl extra-virgin olive oil
2 Tbl parsley, chopped
1 Tbl fresh basil leaves, chopped
1 to 2 cloves garlic, minced
Salt and freshly ground pepper to taste
1 sourdough baguette (about 10oz), diagonally cut into 1/2-inch slices and lightly toasted

In a medium bowl, lightly combine avocados, tomatoes, red onion, olive oil, parsley, basil, garlic, salt and pepper.
Top each slice of toasted bread with about 1 heaping Tbl of the tomato/avocado mixture. Garnish each with a small leaf of basil if desired.

Makes 8 servings.

This recipe is courtesy of the California Avocado Commission.

California Avocado Rings with Prawns

1 Tbl gelatin
1/2 pint chicken stock
3 California avocados
1/2 fresh lemon, juiced
1/2 oz light mayonnaise
1/4 pint double cream
Salt and freshly ground black pepper to taste
8 oz peeled prawns

Place gelatin in a bowl with 4 Tbl cold water and set aside for a few minutes, until it becomes spongy in texture. Heat chicken stock in a medium saucepan over medium/high heat; add gelatin and stir until dissolved completely. Do not allow liquid to boil over or gelatin will become stringy.

Peel, pit and halve avocados, reserving 1/2 for garnish. Mash avocados with lemon juice and add half the mayonnaise, cream, salt and pepper.

Stir in half the gelatin mixture and pour into a 3-pint ring mold. Chill until set. Mix the prawns with the reserved mayonnaise. Empty avocado mold onto serving plate and fill with prawns.

Garnish with avocado slices and serve immediately.

Makes 6 servings.
This recipe is courtesy of the California Avocado Commission.

APPETIZERS

Avocado Stuffed Tomatoes

6 medium tomatoes
Salt to taste
2 medium avocados, peeled, pitted and mashed
2 tsp fresh lemon juice
1 medium onion, chopped finely
1 small can diced green chilies
3 slices vegan bacon, cooked and crumbled
6 lettuce leaves

Slice off the tops of the tomatoes and scoop out pulp, leaving the shells intact. Reserve pulp. Sprinkle a dash of salt inside each tomato shell. Chop reserved pulp finely. Mash avocado fruit and combine with tomato pulp. Mix avocado/tomatoes with lemon juice, onion and diced green chilies.
Stuff tomato shells with avocado mix and sprinkle with bacon. Serve each stuffed tomato on a lettuce leaf.

Makes 6 servings.

Avocado, Cranberry Chutney over Brie

1 (16oz) can whole cranberry sauce
2 Chipotle peppers in adobo sauce, chopped
3/4 c dried cranberries
1 medium apple, peeled, cored and diced
1/4 c granulated sugar
1/4 c brown sugar
1/3 c apple cider vinegar
2 tsp pumpkin pie spice
1 large ripe Haas avocado, peeled, pitted and diced
1 lb round or cut piece of Brie cheese
Crackers, baguette slices or ginger snaps

Preheat oven to 350 degrees F.

Combine cranberry sauce, Chipotle peppers, dried cranberries, apple, sugars, vinegar and pumpkin pie spice in a large saucepan or skillet and cook over medium heat. When mixture begins to bubble, reduce heat to low and simmer for 30 minutes, stirring occasionally. Remove from heat and let cool slightly. Add avocado pieces just before serving.

Place Brie on a shallow oven-safe serving plate (or shallow casserole dish) and pour prepared chutney over cheese.

Place uncovered dish in oven and bake for 5 to 7 minutes, or until cheese is soft, but not melted.

Serve as a spread with crackers, baguette slices or ginger snaps. Makes about 12 servings.

APPETIZERS

Grilled Avocado Quesadilla

6 lbs California avocados
Fresh lime or lemon juice, as needed
Olive oil, as needed
Salt
1 1/2 c Manchego cheese, shredded
1 c Panela cheese, grated
1/2 c Cotija cheese, shredded
Freshly ground black pepper, as needed
12 Poblano peppers, roasted, peeled, cut into thin strips
12 (10-in) flour tortillas
Unsalted butter, as needed
3 c salsa fresca

An hour or two before serving, cut each avocado into 10 or 12 slices, about 3/8-in thick. Brush each slice on both sides with juice, olive oil; lightly sprinkle with salt. Grill, turning once until browned with grill marks; reserve.

Thoroughly mix cheeses; reserve.

Lay one tortilla on work surface. Pour 1/4 c cheese mixture on half the tortilla. On top of cheese, evenly distribute 1/2 oz Poblano strips, about 8. Top with 4 or 5 grilled avocado slices. Drizzle with 1 Tbl salsa; top with 1/4 c cheese mixture. Fold empty tortilla half over ingredients, press lightly.

Brown quesadilla on medium heat in hot butter on both sides. Cover for a minute or so to finish melting cheese. Cut into 4 pieces. Serve with 1/4 c salsa fresca on the side.

Makes 12 servings.

Baked Stuffed California Avocados

2 c diced chicken
1/4 c California sherry
11/2 celery stalks, diced
1/2 c toasted almonds, slivered
1 pimiento, chopped
1/2 c light mayonnaise
2 Tbl fresh lemon juice

Preheat oven to 450 degrees F.
Combine mayonnaise, lemon juice and rind, onion, salt and pepper in a small bowl.
Heat chicken and sherry in a large saucepan. Add celery, almonds, pimiento and the mayonnaise mixture, blending thoroughly.
Place avocado halves on a cookie sheet and fill with mixture. Bake in preheated oven until lightly browned, about 10 minute.
Serve immediately.

Makes 6 servings.

This recipe is courtesy of the California Avocado Commission.

APPETIZERS

Avocados with Mushrooms and Stilton

2 ripe California avocados, halved and "fan" sliced
1 lb mushrooms, sliced
1 Tbl butter, melted
4 slices Stilton cheese, about 1/4-in thick each
4 ramekins or glass Pyrex dishes

Saute mushrooms in butter and divide among 4 dishes. Place a slice of Stilton on each plate of mushrooms. Top each slice with 1/2 California avocado, fan sliced. Brush the avocados with melted butter.

Microwave until cheese just begins to melt, about 45 to 60 seconds. Makes 4 servings.

This recipe is courtesy of the California Avocado Commission.

Avocado Desserts

Avocados have been consumed and enjoyed for centuries and not just in guacamole! Many cultures of the past enjoyed the sweet, velvety flavor of the avocado in drinks and even desserts. South Americans have long considered the avocado an ideal ingredient for a sweet dessert.

At one time avocados were reserved for the tables of royalty only, now they grace a variety of tables all over the world. Most Americans are familiar with the avocado in soups, salads and dips, but many other cultures have enjoyed them in a much sweeter fashion! Brazilians add avocados to their ice cream; Filipinos puree avocados with sugar and milk for a dessert drink and in Latin America avocados are wrapped and given as wedding gifts. Viva Avocado has assembled a group of sweet possibilities.

Avocado Berry Smoothie

1/2 c ice cubes or crushed ice
1 (11.5oz) can peach nectar
1/2 tsp ground cinnamon
1 tsp vanilla extract
1/2 large ripe California avocado, peeled, pitted and cut into large chunks
1 (6oz) carton non-fat vanilla or peach yogurt
1 c fresh blueberries, rinsed picked over and well-drained
1/4 c ripe California avocado, peeled, pitted and sliced lengthwise for garnish
6 plump blueberries (optional) for garnish

Place all ingredients in a blender with lid. Blend on high for 2 minutes, or until smooth and creamy. Pour into 2 tall glasses to serve. Pierce slice of avocado with 3 blueberries with cocktail sword or skewer and hang on side of glass for garnish.

Makes 2 servings.

This recipe is courtesy of the California Avocado Commission.

DESSERT

Avocado Holiday Cake

1 egg, slightly beaten
1/2 c mashed avocado
1/2 c buttermilk
1 c pecans, chopped
1 c candied cherries, chopped
1 c candied pineapple, chopped
2 c sifted all-purpose flour
3/4 c sugar
1/2 tsp baking soda
1/2 tsp baking powder
1/4 tsp salt

Preheat oven to 350 degrees F.

Mix egg, avocado, buttermilk, pecans, cherries and pineapple. In a large bowl mix flour, sugar, baking soda, baking powder and salt. Pour avocado mixture into flour mixture and mix only until flour is moistened. Do not over mix.

Pour into well-greased 9x13-inch pan or 3 4x7-inch loaf pans. Fill slightly more than half full. Bake 1 hour for large pan or 45 minutes for small loaf pans. Cool on rack.

Makes 24 servings.

Blender Avocado Cheesecake

1 California avocado, peeled and pitted
8 oz cream cheese, softened
1/2 c sour cream
3 lemon peel strips
3 3/4 oz vanilla-flavored instant pudding and pie filling
1 graham cracker crust

Blend together avocado, cream cheese, sour cream and lemon peel in an electric blender until smooth. Add pudding and blend until just mixed. Pour into crust and chill several hours until set.

Makes 1 pie.

This recipe is courtesy of the California Avocado Commission.

DESSERT

Avocado Mousse Dessert

1 envelope (2 1/4 tsp) unflavored gelatin
1/2 c cold water
2 ripe Haas avocados, peeled, pitted and cubed
2 Tbl fresh orange juice
1/2 c lukewarm water
1 1/2 c low-fat sour cream, room temperature or warmed slightly
1/2 c sugar
1 Tbl vanilla extract
2 Tbl fresh orange juice
Zest of one orange
Oil for preparing mold pan
Fresh raspberries and candied walnuts for garnish

Sprinkle gelatin over cold water in a heavy saucepan and let stand 1 minute. Cook over low heat for 1 to 2 minutes, remove from heat and let cool completely.

Place avocados in a blender or food processor and while blending add 2 Tbl orange juice and up to 1/2 c water, blending until mixture is smooth and creamy.

Transfer to a large bowl and gently whisk gelatin into mixture until gelatin is completely incorporated.

In a separate bowl, blend sour cream, sugar, vanilla, orange juice and orange zest until smooth.

Gently fold sour cream mixture into avocado mixture; mix well until smooth and creamy.

Lightly oil gelatin mold (should be 3 to 4 cup capacity).

Pour mixture into mold and smooth the top. Cover with plastic wrap and chill mold until firm, at least 4 hours to overnight.

Slice to serve and garnish each serving with fresh raspberries and candied walnuts.

Makes 12 to 16 servings.

California Avocado Ice Cream
With Hazelnut Shards

Ice Cream Ingredients
4 egg yolks
3/4 c sugar
2 c milk
1/2 c whipping cream
5 medium ripe California avocados
2 tsp fresh lime juice
1 tsp fresh lemon juice

Hazelnut shards Ingredients
2 1/4 c sugar
5 Tbl water
3/4 c hazelnuts, skinned, toasted and coarsely chopped

To make ice cream, beat yolks and sugar until ribbons form; reserve. Heat milk to boiling, stirring frequently. Temper reserved egg mixture with a little hot milk; stir tempered mixture into remaining hot milk.

Heat mixture over low heat to 185 degrees F, stirring constantly.

Remove from heat and continue to stir, slowly adding cream.

Thoroughly chill mixture.

Meanwhile, pit and peel avocados. Puree in food processor with lime and lemon juices. Whisk avocado puree into chilled custard. Freeze in an ice cream maker following manufacturers instructions. Store in an airtight container in freezer.

To make hazelnut shards, mix sugar and water in a heavy saucepan. Over medium/low heat cook sugar and water without stirring until water evaporates and sugar turns golden brown, about 10 minutes. Working quickly, stir in finely chopped nuts. Immediately, thinly spread mixture on a buttered sheet pan. Cool and then break into shards.

Garnish each ice cream serving with hazelnut shards.

Makes 4 servings.

This recipe is courtesy of the California Avocado Commission.

DESSERT

Avocado Banana Dessert

5 ripe avocados, peeled, pitted and mashed
3 to 4 bananas, cut into chunks
4 Tbl sugar
2 lemons, juiced
Fresh raspberries to garnish

Peel, pit and coarsely mash avocados. Mash bananas and mix with avocados. Mix in sugar and lemon juice. Chill for 30 minutes before serving. Garnish each serving with fresh raspberries.

Makes 8 to 10 servings.

Persian Cream with Pistachio Nuts

2 California avocados, halved and peeled
1/4 c fresh lime or lemon juice
1 1/2 c confectioners sugar
1 1/2 c roasted shelled pistachio nuts
2 Tbl crème de cacao
2 c heavy cream, whipped
lime slices for garnish

Puree avocados with lime juice, sugar, nuts and crème de cacao until smooth. Fold into whipping cream.
Spoon into serving dishes or into avocado shells.

Makes 6 servings.

This recipe is courtesy of the California Avocado Commission.

DESSERT

Avocado Ice Cream

2 c whole milk
3/4 c white sugar
3 strips fresh orange zest
Pinch of salt
2 Tbl cornstarch
2 ripe-firm avocados, peeled, pitted and cut into chunks
1/2 orange, juiced
Ice Cream Maker

Bring 13/4 c milk, 1/2 c sugar, zest and a pinch of salt to a simmer in a 2-quart heavy saucepan over moderate heat. Whisk together cornstarch and remaining 1/4 c milk in a small bowl until smooth and whisk into simmering milk. Bring to a boil, whisking constantly, boiling for 1 minute.
Transfer mixture to a metal bowl and then place it in a larger bowl of ice and cold water. Cool completely, stirring frequently. Discard zest.
In a blender, puree avocados, orange juice and remaining 1/4 c sugar until smooth. Add milk mixture and blend well.
Freeze avocado mixture using an ice cream maker and transfer to an airtight container. Freeze until hardened, about 1 hour.

Makes about 1 quart

Avocado Sorbet

1 c sugar
1 c light corn syrup
2 c water
1 tsp grated lime peel
3 ripe avocados, peeled, pitted and mashed
2 Tbl lemon juice
1 Tbl lime juice
Fresh raspberries and cookie crisps

Bring sugar, corn syrup and water to boil in a large saucepan. Remove from heat and stir in lime peel. Cool for 50 to 60 minutes.

Blend avocados, lemon and lime juices in food processor or blender until smooth. Add cooked sugar mixture and blend again until smooth. Pour into a 13x9-inch pan or two smaller pans, so depth is about 1/2 inch. Freeze one hour.

Remove sorbet from freezer and then beat for 1 to 2 minutes until mixture is light and creamy.

Pour back into pan and cover with plastic wrap. Freeze until firm, about 4 hours. Serve sorbet with fresh raspberries and cookie crisps.

Makes 1 to 2 cups.

DESSERT

Dear Readers

As a 35 year, veteran vegetarian and health-food fanatic, I can attest to the wide range of positive effects, mentally and physically, a healthy diet can induce. As a parent, I have involved my own children in food preparation and planning, teaching by example how to prepare and eat a diet rich in taste and nutrients. Mornings usually consist of fresh fruits mixed into oatmeals and cereals and evenings are always full of freshly cut vegetables, within creative combinations of wholesome meals. We have fun in the kitchen, always searching for new ways to add spice and find interesting, delicious combinations of our favorite ingredients. It isn't a chore in our house to eat our fruits and veggies; it is a way of life. I hope our readers can do the same.

—Nicholas Webb, Author and Health-Food Junkie

Index